MAKING CONNECTIONS

Getting things done
with other people

Making

Connections

Getting Things Done
With Other People

Nico Swaan
Erik Boers

Illustrations by
Joost Tennekes, pure&simple, Amsterdam

bookshaker

First Published In Great Britain 2012
by www.BookShaker.com

© Copyright Nico Swaan and Erik Boers

Praise

"Only just appeared and already a classic. This book is the expression of an oral tradition among management educators and trainers that is now almost six decades old, and that has transformed the way we lead, interact and do business. The same tradition has discovered the importance of having a vision and inspiring others, and it has helped countless leaders to be better listeners and express themselves more fully. I am immensely grateful to Swaan and Boers that all of this is now available to a wider audience."

Erik de Haan,
Director of Centre for Coaching,
Ashridge, U.K.

"One of the first things that a professional needs to learn in his/her career is that there is a difference between being right and successfully convincing the business environment that you are – a difficult process. In the ever-increasing complexity of business environments it takes years to master the art of the constructive influencing of others. The development programme underlying this book has proved over a decade to accelerate the learning process of NXP employees all around the globe and has thus improved the quality of communication and co-operation in the company. This book is an inspiring source of material for everyone who wants to increase their personal effectiveness in influencing others."

Ellen van Bommel
HRM Central R&D Design Services
NXP Semiconductors, The Netherlands

"The material in this book creates insights into one's personal style of communicating and how this might impact on others. The concepts and models stimulate the development of style flexibility and therefore communication effectiveness."

Hanneke Kusters
Learning & Development Advisor
Mars Nederland, The Netherlands.

"If it is about effective use of your influence in the work context then I gladly recommend *Making Connections* by Nico Swaan and Erik Boers. In their book they manage to bring together and interweave major themes like Communication, Trust and Influence in a very recognisable and logical manner. The book provides an understandable theoretical framework as well as numerous practical methods and tools with which the reader can determine his or her own preferred style, blind spots and most useful approaches to developing more effective influence behaviour."

Leonoor van Gils
Senior Advisor HRD Training & Development
Randstad Nederland bv
The Netherlands

"Making Connections is a very powerful book. The models used by the authors have proven their value in large organisations and big multinationals, where communication regularly breaks down and trust evaporates. In very straightforward and accessible language Nico Swaan and Erik Boers describe what happens in the workplace, and how daily communication can be brought to a higher level. Clear examples are given of getting your own message across, switching off yourself and opening up for the agenda of others, and dealing with each other in a mutually respectful way marked by trust and connection. I have used the models for years now in my work, and will keep doing so."

Frank Garten
Intercultural Consultant
Utrecht, The Netherlands.

"Reading this book reminded me of my participation in one of the first ever Focus on Influence programmes. It was probably the most impactful training I have received in my professional life. Ultimately, personal performance and effective influencing are seamlessly connected. Certainly in today's complex and modern organisations, where working together closely is essential for growth, quality and satisfaction."

Barteld van der Weerd
Regional Marketing Director Western Europe
Esselte Corporation,
The Netherlands

"This book is about an oh so important and at the same time oh so difficult quality/skill, which all kinds of people, if not indeed everyone, can develop to his or her advantage. The central theme of the book is that making connections with and influencing others effectively requires more than the flexible use of three different 'dimensions' of influence behaviour. It is also about trust (simple, blind and authentic), the various levels of communication, and about non-verbal communication. The book constantly challenges the reader to experiment and reflect, and is clearly the wonderful outcome of the authors' many years of experience."

Sjaak Evers
(Former) Global Quality Manager, Philips Electronics
Supporter of the Rhineland way of organising
The Netherlands

Having attended a training programme based on the models and concepts described in this book, participants wrote that these:
"...are just like a set of new keys to open doors that people don't even realize can be opened – or even exist. With some practice – it's not magic, you need to work on it – approaching difficult situations in daily life at home or at work will feel a much lighter undertaking."

Olivier Piron,
Project and Sports Manager
Switzerland

"...formed a transformative experience during which I learned to better apply my abilities to make team accomplishments more effective and, even more importantly, meaningful."

Adam Miller
Sales Director
Cree, Inc., USA

"... were simple, easy to use, and adaptive to various country cultural contexts and settings. The models avoid jargon and simply focus on the people that matter: You, We and I."

Bala Asirvatham
Senior Regional Human Resources Manager
Navteq Europe B.V., The Netherlands

"...made me re-realise the fundamental importance of human communication and perhaps even more importantly the vast number of forms that communication may take, whether intentional or not."

Paul Harrison
Contract DfT Engineer
Wolfson Microelectronics

CONTENTS

FOREWORD

This book is a thoughtful and complete exposition of the theory and practice underlying an extremely creative and successful programme for training individuals to be effective in the day to day interpersonal and group situations faced by members of all organisations. Building soundly on sixty years of pioneering theory and practice in applied psychology by others and by themselves, the authors have created elegant and powerful processes that anyone can use to enhance their personal power and influence. They have been exceptionally generous in sharing publicly what many would regard as proprietary information, and for this reason the book will be of particular interest to management educators and training professionals, as well as the interested layman.

Roger Harrison
Whidbey Island, Washington
Author,
The Collected Papers of Roger Harrison, McGraw-Hill, 1995
Consultant's Journey, McGraw-Hill, 1995

Authors' preface

Towards the end of 1997 we were approached by an industrial client who asked whether we could develop an influencing skills programme for the sales division as well as for the people in the factory. Given our many years of experience in the areas of communication skills training and consulting, we gladly accepted the challenge. In 1998 we delivered the first version of a four-day training programme which came to be known as *Focus on Influence*. Since then the programme has taken on a definite structure and design, and is provided to various organisations throughout the world. Participants are introduced to the different "dimensions of behaviour" which it is necessary to master in order to carry out a good business discussion: the *I-dimension*, the *You-dimension*, and the *We-dimension*. Each of these dimensions is necessary in order to achieve results when working in close cooperation with others. During the programme we work exclusively with the participants' own real-life situations. This ensures that the programme is both confronting and applicable in practice.

Now, almost fifteen years since we started, we wish, with this book, to make the theory and exercises which have proven their worth, available to everyone. We address ourselves to professionals who seek to work on personal development, to leaders who are interested in the development of themselves and their people, and to trainers, coaches and consultants who train, guide and facilitate others in conducting crucial discussions.

In the introduction of our book we show a little bit of how much we owe to the work of our predecessors, of whom Roger Harrison stands out and has been so kind as to write a preface. We wish to make special mention of Ruud Olthoff and Piet Breed, who were instrumental in the development of early versions of both the influence model (described in Chapter 2) and the *Focus on Influence* programme. We also thank our *Learning Consortium* colleagues. In conducting programmes with them over the years, we have tested and fine-tuned the theories and many of the exercises in this book. They and others, including former participants, have read various versions of this book and provided extremely useful commentary. We also acknowledge with gratitude the many hundreds of participants, from all over the world, upon whose enthusiastic participation and experimentation we have capitalised.

Finally, we thank Lucy McCarraher and Roger Woodham at Bookshaker for their warm encouragement, and their skilful editing of our manuscript.

Nico Swaan
Erik Boers
Hilversum/Eindhoven
December 2011

INTRODUCTION

How do you ensure that you achieve the desired results in a conversation? Conducting a good conversation is an extremely complex process. Though we all do it all the time, it can and does happen that you leave a meeting with a sense of dissatisfaction. You have a sense that you were not so much persuading anyone as talking to yourself. Like a misunderstood prophet you scattered the seeds of your wisdom on the barren earth around you. Or you got the impression from the reactions of others that they felt attacked rather than persuaded. With your sharp tongue you focused on what was wrong with their proposals and arguments. Maybe you were left with a sense of having been forced to back down under the pressure of their arguments. You missed opportunities without being able to say exactly where they were.

Working with this book

To help you come to grips with a "good conversation" this book examines its various dimensions and components. This will help you to analyse your own behaviour, to identify your preferences and automatic responses and thereby to discover where there is scope for increasing your effectiveness when influencing others. This in turn will make it possible to make conscious decisions about which behaviour to use. The core of this book takes the form of a three-dimensional influence model. Observation of our own and others' discussions has made clear that it is necessary to be able to move freely among the behaviours included in the following three dimensions:

- The *I-dimension*: providing direction with clear proposals, demands, reasoning, promises and judgments;
- The *You-dimension*: inviting the other to share his or her ideas, insights, and experiences;
- The *We-dimension*: building trust by relating to the other at the personal level of feelings and underlying needs.

What do these dimensions and behaviours look and sound like? With which are you comfortable, and with which are you not? What is the impact of the various dimensions and behaviours? Are you able to switch comfortably from one to the other? How can you best respond to the behaviour of the other person? You will find answers to these questions in this book. The key lies in increasing your own flexibility and effectiveness, but without losing yourself in myriad "tricks". Be yourself, and become increasingly true to yourself. You achieve this by relying less on your automatic pilot and more on making conscious decisions in choosing the behaviours which suit you in the different situations in which you find yourself.

Background of the influence model
Influence behaviours
Our model builds on the work of Roger Harrison and David Berlew in the 1970s. These social scientists met each other at the *National Training Laboratories*, the cradle of many later communication skills training programmes.

Both were dissatisfied with the fact that available training material and methodology in the area of communication skills was based entirely on values such as "openness", "trust", and "authenticity". In their view, people in organisations needed a far broader behavioural repertoire in order to exercise influence. The preference which had developed after the Second World War for participative leadership had, for them, swung too far towards a reverence for soft, friendly styles of influence. They recognised that successful individuals in organisations did far more than listen and be open and honest: they argued for points of view, they levelled frank criticism, they negotiated, they committed themselves to specific results, they said "no" to certain assignments, and they inspired and encouraged others. Harrison and Berlew decided to develop a training programme in which individuals would have the opportunity to develop their skills in as wide a range of different behaviours as possible.

They began by observing and coding all the behaviours which seemed to be instrumental in business conversations. This eventually led to the *Positive Power and Influence* (PPI) model.[1]

Hard, Competitive Styles		Soft, Co-operative Styles	
Rewards and Punishments	**Assertive Persuasion**	**Participation and Trust**	**Common Vision**
Assertive, demanding behaviours	Reasoning behaviours	Trust-building behaviours	Inspirational behaviours

---

[1] Roger Harrison: *Consultant's Journey*, 1995: 80

3

In order to influence others in the organisational setting all these styles were considered necessary. The model presumed to be inclusive, to cover all possible types of behaviour as they occur in conversations. In this way, the model offered a method of analysing and describing verbal behaviour: which style is being used, and what is its effect? It also provides an opportunity to analyse which behaviours an individual masters effectively, and with which behaviours he or she could profitably experiment.

We simplified and supplemented the influence model developed by Harrison and Berlew. Instead of four styles we use three "dimensions" of influence behaviour and have given them neutral names. Our experience has shown this to be sufficient to describe the basic "movements" which people make when attempting to influence each other.

- The *I-dimension*: you seek to be heard, and to formulate clearly what you think and want.
- The *You-dimension*: you take a step back and invite the other to convey what he or she thinks, wants or feels.
- The *We-dimension*: you place yourself beside the other, acknowledge the other and his experience, and share your own feelings and needs – with the intent of creating a productive, trusting relationship.

In these three dimensions it is easy to recognise the styles used in the PPI. The "hard" styles, including "Reward and Punishment" and "Assertive Persuasion" fall under our *I-dimension*, where we also place what in PPI language is called "Common Vision", because this style also centres on the leader's perspective: she or he seeks to make clear and attractive something which is based on shared values. The two "soft styles" in PPI language are split between two distinct dimensions: the *You* and the *We*.

In our view this last dimension is particularly worth noting. Whereas Berlew in particular placed a heavy accent on inspirational leadership, leading to the identification of the Common Vision style, we emphasise the importance of trust and openness in today's knowledge-based organisations, focused as we are on the process of "making connections". Having said that, the exact form of a model with styles or dimensions is, in our view, of secondary importance: a model needs to be easily understood, to "map out" the whole range of possible influence behaviours, and provide a framework which allows participants to explore and experiment in such a way that they can discover where their key development opportunities lie.

Speech acts

While giving form to the "three dimensions" we have not based ourselves only on our own observations, but have also gained inspiration from the studies in the philosophy of language published by John Searle[2]. Searle was concerned to find the rules which govern our use of language: which speech acts can be found in all human languages? What *do* we do when we speak? What *can* you do with words?

Searle moved forward from the work of his teacher J.L. Austin. Austin had introduced the notion of "illocutionary acts". According to Austin, in a speech act the following happens:

---

[2]John Searle: *Speech Acts*, 1969. Chapter 3

5

a. someone states certain words,
b. he refers to something or expresses a value judgement
    about something,
c. in doing so he harbours a certain intention (he wishes to
    promise something, to criticize someone, to demonstrate
    something).

Austin claimed that there are thousands of expressions for
these intentions, these illocutionary acts. Searle tried to
classify Austin's illocutionary acts and came up with five
categories:

1. Assertive: focused on stating the truth (All seats for this
    flight are booked. I can demonstrate that we will lose
    market share. A synthetic component will last longer than
    one made of metal.)
2. Directive: focused on leading to an action by the other.
    (Let's give that idea a try. I insist that you participate.
    Give me three minutes.)
3. Commissive: focused on committing the speaker to some
    future act. (I will do it. I won't be able to get to that now.)
4. Expressive: focused on conveying the speaker's state of
    mind. (I'm sorry. Great to see you. My condolences.)
5. Declarative: focused on defining the situation. (You have
    been accepted. The ball is out. What you did there was
    unacceptable. From now we will focus all of our energy on
    our three main clients.)

We have regrouped Searle's classification into the three
dimensions and made several additions. We have replaced the
term "illocutionary act" with the notion of "commitment",

following Fernando Flores, a Chilean engineer, philosopher, entrepreneur and politician who studied under Searle in California.[3] We discovered Flores' work through our colleague George Simons who studied under him and then simplified the language and the concepts into the form in which we now use them. Simons worked intensively with individuals and organisations seeking forms of cross-cultural communication which were less liable to misunderstandings.[4]

Each dimension gives expression to an intention and defines a commitment.

I-dimension: what I say is true, appropriate and correct. I stand by what I say.

You-dimension: I take what you have to say seriously; I do my best to understand you and am open to having what you say reflect in what I think and feel.

We-dimension: I drop my mask, and trust that you will not seek to hurt me. I stand side-by-side with you and I will not hurt you.

The five acts which Searle identified fall within two of our three dimensions: assertive, directive, commissive and declarative fall within the *I-dimension*. Expressive acts fall within the *We-dimension*, which we have extended with two additional behaviours related to the experience of feelings. In addition to expressing or sharing one's own feelings we include disclosing the (un)fulfilled needs which lie behind feelings, as

---

[3]Fernando Flores: *Management and Communication in the Office of the Future* (typescript in the possession of the authors)

[4]George Simons, Working Together – *How to become More Effective in a Multicultural Organization*, 1989: 37

well as acknowledging and empathising with the feelings of others.

Perhaps remarkably, Searle provides no room for asking questions or listening. He sees asking questions as a variation of directive behaviour, namely a call to provide available information: "I request that you tell me about ..." Indeed, questions are often used – and misused – for this purpose. But Searle does real listening little justice. "Asking" includes assuming an inviting posture, demonstrating the intent to take your words seriously and not just to hear you out. The same is true for paraphrasing as a part of (active) listening: this is not a form of arguing but an activity designed to check whether you have indeed understood someone. We have included these behaviours in the *You-dimension*.

Outline of this book

Why have all those discussions? Can't we do with a little less talking? In order to understand what constitutes a good discussion you first need to understand the wide variety of needs which underpin our seemingly never-ending desire to meet with others and discuss things. Only if people's underlying needs are met will they leave a discussion feeling good. Chapter 1 examines this matter.

After a careful look at the behaviours included in the three-dimensional model in Chapter 2 we focus our attention on a crucial concept when it comes to working together effectively: *trust*. Your ability to influence others stands or falls on the measure of trust, which you enjoy. If others do not trust you it is extremely difficult to influence them about anything. How do you regain trust if it appears lost? How do you build a trusting relationship? What is the difference between trust and reliability? These questions are addressed in Chapter 3.

With a task-focused orientation you offer people new insights. That is fortunate, too, because in the end that is what it is all about. Problems have to be resolved, ideas have to be worked out and objectives must be realised. However, all of us regularly experience meetings during which little progress is made on matters of task or content. The discussion breaks down, gets repetitive or goes around in circles. The time is then right to intervene on one of the other levels of communication: procedure, interaction and climate. Perhaps there is confusion about the procedure being followed. Or the discussions become marked by attack and defence patterns. Maybe all manner of negative feelings are playing a dominant role in the background, with the result that nobody is prepared to make a conciliatory gesture. It is important to develop an understanding of all these levels in our communication so that you can trust that your contribution will be directed at the appropriate level. Chapter 4 examines these levels.

What you say is important; of perhaps equal importance is how you say it. No language is as influential as body language. The sound of your voice, your facial expression, the posture and movements of your body play a dominant role. You can influence others with your body language without being aware of it and perhaps against your will. Your voice can sound sharper or softer than you intended, a smile driven by uncertainty can seriously undermine your message, or you fail to look at the other person in a way which holds attention. It also works the other way around: with their impressive stature, soothing voice or vicious demeanour others exert greater influence over you than you wish. Feelings of anxiety or enthusiasm take charge of you and strongly limit your behaviour. What is going on with our thoughts and feelings? To what extent can we control them? What can you surmise from the body language of others? Is it possible to work on your own non-verbal behaviour? We look at this aspect of interpersonal communication in Chapter 5.

Many things play a role simultaneously in each discussion: three dimensions, four levels, verbal and non-verbal behaviour. How do you learn to acquire a keener sense of all this? How do you learn to make your own behaviour more flexible and more effective? How can you develop an influencing style which "fits" you? In order to challenge you to experiment with new behaviour and to reflect on the sources of your behavioural patterns, each chapter ends with a section *Experimenting and Reflecting*.

We end the book by looking back and reporting on the learning experiences of former participants. These provide some insight into what behavioural learning is fundamentally about. We also briefly review our experiences with the influence model in Asia and the Far East. This is relevant, because we, in the West, are increasingly confronted with clients, suppliers, colleagues and leaders/managers from those regions. To what extent can you be successful in those countries with our way of influencing others?

All the lessons in this book are brought together in Appendix 3: a checklist with twelve questions which can help you to prepare for a difficult conversation. Convincing others begins with convincing yourself that you are well prepared.

1

WHY DO WE TALK

SO MUCH?

We do talk a lot. Life is dominated by talking with others, at home, at play and particularly at work, which appears to be a good thing. When people do not connect with each other and talk to each other, whether it is socially, in political, religious, community or civic organisations, or in the workplace, then the economy, democracy and even individuals' health and happiness suffer.[5] Children who later do well at school are talked to up to two-and-a-half times more than children who later struggle at school.[6] People are not "brought up" so much as "talked up". To most of humankind, almost nothing seems quite as natural as talking. A good conversation is one of the most valuable aspects of life.

---

[5]Robert D. Putnam, *Bowling Alone: The Collapse and Revival of American Community*, 2000.

[6]David Brooks: *The Social Animal*, 2011. Page 106

In my view engaging in conversation is one of the most useful and natural exercises for the mind. I find it the most pleasant of life's occupations and that is why, if I were forced to make a choice at this moment, I would rather lose the power of sight than my hearing or my tongue.

Michel de Montaigne, 1586

More recently, modern British philosopher, Michael Oakshott, wrote: "Conversation distinguishes the human being from the animal and the civilized man from the barbarian."[7]

How we feel about talking is, however, distinctly ambivalent. At work there are endless meetings and conference calls, and even emails are a form of "talking". Sometimes people in organisations sigh, and mutter: "Why do we talk so much? Can't we just roll up our sleeves and get something done?" They get tired just thinking about all those meetings. Meetings can also generate uncertainty: "In addition to standing out at my work, I also have to be able to vanquish the tigers in the meeting room."

Getting something done, however, is almost always a matter of working *together*; of cooperating with others. Activities need to be coordinated, individuals need to take each other into account and they need to answer to each other for plans formulated and results achieved. Talking from a place of connection with one another is an absolute necessity. People are social animals. As a person you are (*esse*) always among (*inter*) other people – with diverging *interests*. A person seeks connection in diversity, and that is done by talking.

---

[7]In: Stephen Miller, *Conversation, a history of a declining art*, 2006: ix

Talking and Listening

At the same time, talking to good effect can be extremely difficult. Talking to nobody, talking into empty space, is seen as a symptom of a serious disorder. Yet people frequently feel as if they are talking to themselves, or to a wall. What is said just doesn't appear to "land" on the other person. It has no impact, makes no difference to anything, and doesn't influence anybody. There is no connection; it may indeed feel like talking into a telephone after the line has gone dead.

Talking only makes sense if someone else is listening.

What was really incomprehensible was the discussion, as it was called. The people spoke perfectly past one another. Constantly they said they understood each other, answered each other. But it wasn't so. No one, not a single one of the discussants, showed the slightest indication of a change of mind in view of the reasons presented. That's how it always is. Saying something to another: how can we expect it to affect anything? The current of thoughts, images and feelings that flows through us on every side, has such force that it would be a miracle if it didn't simply sweep away and consign to oblivion all words anyone else says to us, if they didn't by accident, sheer accident, suit our own words. Is it different with me? I thought. Did I really listen to anybody else? Let him into me with his words so that my internal current would be diverted? I had found it eerie how everybody had been talking only to themselves.

This could be an eloquent eulogy to yet another futile business meeting, one in which no one was connecting with anyone else.

But this almost tragic text comes from a quite different source. It was written in reference to a (fictional) discussion situated in All Souls College, Oxford![8]

Conversations in Organisations

At work, as elsewhere, people value a good conversation. A bad or uninteresting conversation is exhausting and disappointing because it fails to meet a basic need. If you wish to influence someone you have to make sure they feel that they have had an interesting, nourishing conversation, which motivated, stimulated and inspired. Individuals meet, get to know one another and during the conversation get to know themselves better. While getting acquainted, they generate new knowledge; insights complement each other, unfamiliar backgrounds come to the foreground, feelings are shared, dreams become palpable. Business conversations usually seek to follow a structure as follows:

- Introduction: creating trust, putting each at ease
- Opening: determining the objective
- Inquiry: getting the facts on the table, discovering the perceptions of all participants regarding the matter at hand, uncovering underlying needs
- Solution: formulating proposals, putting them side-by-side, selecting
- Follow-up: planning next steps
- Closing: review of meeting, taking leave

---

[8]Pascal Mercier, *Night Train to Lisbon*, 2008. Page 136.

Things can go wrong during each of these phases: mutual trust can fail to materialise, objectives can remain unclear, the inquiry is incomplete, proposals can fail to connect with the issue at hand, next steps are not taken, the close is hurried and people leave with a sense of having missed something. But if the meeting has gone well then trust has been created, participants feel focused on a shared objective, the world has been mapped out and is better understood, proposals have been formulated which no one could have thought of by himself, realistic action steps have been planned and everyone leaves with a sense of satisfaction and looking forward to meeting again the next time.

Cooperation requires coordination of effort. That is one of the most important reasons for all the meetings at work. Working is working together and working together is communicating. Meetings have become an essential means of production in addition to labour, materials and capital. That is more so now than in the past. Five developments have contributed to this:

1. Flatter organisation structures;
2. Multi-disciplinary teams;
3. Teams spread across diverse locations;
4. Increased business contacts with different cultures;
5. Increasing independence of professionals who do not appreciate "being told".

Cutting out layers of management has meant that in addition to their operational tasks, more controlling responsibilities have ended up with employees. They cannot focus themselves solely on the task but also need to keep regulatory systems working, such as planning, maintenance, stock control and contacts with clients and suppliers. All this requires constant consultation. Multi-disciplinary teams are proliferating because products and services are becoming increasingly complex. Working together with other disciplines requires particularly careful consultation because not everyone shares the same professional background or "speaks the same language". Such teams are also frequently spread across various locations, cities or even countries. This in turn requires more formal meetings because team members do not meet each other in the corridors. Globalisation has also meant that language and cultural barriers have moved into the foreground. Colleagues, managers, employees, clients and suppliers come from different countries and regions. Effort is required to meet and get to know and understand the backgrounds of foreign colleagues. As project manager or team leader you cannot make do with email messages; you will need to send powerful and convincing (verbal) messages.

Conversation forms the binding agent and lubricant in the wheels of an organisation. That makes conversation neither more than, nor less than, a means of production; a means, which helps to speed up and facilitate production itself. But in many organisations conversation is even more than a means of production. It is an inextricable part of the product or service which is delivered. There can be no law firm, consultancy or financial service without conversation. In the hotel and catering industry and in healthcare, personal conversations form a key ingredient of what is delivered. Many material products are also sold because of the stories which accompany them (beautiful, comfortable, sexy, sporty, reliable, handy, healthy, exclusive, simple, etc..). How a product is talked about is at least as important as its functionality.

Do what you say and say what you do

When someone in an organisation calls out: "Do something! Action!", then that means: "get something moving, get to work." Being action-oriented often means the showing of initiative. That is what managers mean when they say, "I wish my people would do more!" They mean: show initiative, stop avoiding responsibility, come up with creative solutions. Talking is essential. Actions are not things which just happen, but are the deeds or operations which stem from someone's initiative, behind which resides an intention. It becomes clear that it is not just a routine operation but a well thought through action when it is explained and justified; when it is talked about.

There is a particular tendency among people with a technical background to think: "Let my actions speak for themselves! There is no great need to talk about things." Unfortunately for them good work does not always speak for itself. It does not draw automatic attention to itself; it simply ensures that someone else has something less to worry about. Before you know it, good work is seen as normal work. You run the risk of being seen by your manager as an eager beaver: give you a job to do and you sink your teeth into it. If we do not tell our story then others will not realise how much we have had to take the initiative in order to achieve something. There will be little or no recognition. It is important to "Talk the walk" as well as to "Walk the talk".

When people are able to explain their actions, the value of

their efforts can be judged, and they can be recognised as initiators and entrepreneurs. When you talk about and explain your work you will be recognised as a fellow human rather than as a workhorse. It is necessary not only to do what you have said/promised, but to say what you have done.

Discussions make sense

Frequently you only realise which choices you have made in the course of your professional actions when someone stops to ask you about them. Of course you are in constant conversation with yourself about the steps you will follow, but you also take steps unconsciously. If others force you to reflect on what you have done it becomes clear that there was more behind the actions than you realised.

This is the way Socrates went to work twenty-five centuries ago in Athens. He approached civic and army leaders, merchants and teachers and asked them about the beliefs and opinions from which their actions came. His student Plato recorded these discussions in his famous *Dialogues*. In the course of their encounters, Socrates' discussion partners discovered that their beliefs and opinions were not infallible. His questions forced them to develop more careful perceptions of themselves and the world around them. Plato continued these discussions in the Academy after Socrates' death. The Academy was the spawning ground of philosophy and science in our Western culture.

A similar fundamental examination takes place if you enter into discussion with your colleagues about your decisions, your professional beliefs and ideals. You acquire a view on the wider context. What are you doing? Why does that occupy your attention and time so much? What is it about that which is so important? This is a valuable form of discussion in organisations. An organisation is fundamentally a group of people united around an idea ("connecting people", "sense and simplicity", "science for a better life"). If we no longer understand or buy in to that idea then we lose direction as well as motivation.

Discussions help to make sense of our world and our activities; they give them meaning. "Meetings make sense", as organisational psychologist Karl Weick once put it.[9]

To summarise, a good discussion is important in organisations because:

- People are the heart of the organisation and people are talkers; they talk (and listen) in order to feel connected, because people are social animals;
- It is ever less possible to work as a soloist, so we constantly have to talk to others in order to coordinate work and seek solutions together;
- Talking is, in itself, in many cases, that which professionals deliver in today's organisations;
- Our actions cannot be valued properly if we do not explain them.

It is through discussions with others that we can determine whether that which occupies us makes sense.

If you wish to influence others and also enjoy the discussions in which you take part then you will have to do justice to these needs: connection, coordination, contribution, recognition, sense; needs which drive you and the person with whom you are in discussion.

---

[9]Karl E. Weick, *Sensemaking in Organizations*. 1995: 185

Experimentation and Reflection

Looking back...

In order to gain insight into your effectiveness in discussions, consider the following questions related to the last twenty-four hours or so of your life.

- To whom did you talk?
- What happened while you were talking?
- What did you do well? Why?
- What was the added value of the discussion?
- Which needs were met during the discussion (connection, coordination, contribution, recognition, sense)? Which not?
- What was the purpose of the discussion, the intention – from your point of view? From the point of view of the other?
- In your view, was this purpose achieved? In the other's view?
- What did the other do well?
- To what are you going to pay more attention in the future?

Make a few notes for yourself based on these questions, and start to reflect regularly on the effect of talking in the work context, and on the effectiveness of your own talking.

When it threatens to go wrong[10]

According to folk wisdom: *If you're in danger of "losing it", first count to ten.*

The problem for many of us is that when we find ourselves in a stressful situation we lose our composure and continue

---

[10]Derived from Rick Ross: "Moments of Awareness". In: Peter Senge *et.al.*: *The Fifth Discipline Fieldbook*, 1994. Pages 216-218.

with the same behaviour that got us into difficulties in the first place.

This reflection is designed to help you to take a psychological time out and reflect on the discussion which you feel isn't going as you would wish. It can help you to remain in charge of the situation when irritation, anger or frustration threaten to gain the upper hand. It is possible to make a habit of this exercise. It is based on the following steps. Ask yourself:

What is happening, right now? Continue by asking the following questions:

1. What am I doing, right now?
   What am I feeling, right now?
   What am I thinking, right now?
2. What do I want, right now? What am I trying to achieve at this moment?
3. What am I doing, right now, that is preventing me from achieving what I want?
4. What would be the best thing for me to do, right now?

The following example might clarify:

What is happening?
"I'm stuck in a confrontation and it's not getting anywhere."

What am I doing?
"I'm being very assertive and putting the other person under a lot of pressure."

How do I feel?
"I'm getting angry."

What are my thoughts?
"I think he just doesn't want to listen ... or else he's stupid."

What do I want? (Try to answer this question in the positive rather than with "I don't want...")
"I want him to understand my worries. It's not easy to explain. Actually, maybe I'm getting all wound up because I'm not as well prepared as I should be. I've let him take the brunt of my anger with myself."

What am I doing which is preventing me from getting what I want?
"Well, I'm just putting him under as much pressure as I can."

What would be the best thing for to do right now?
"Maybe if I offer my apologies we can move on."

Take a personal situation from the recent past as an example. Answer the four questions for yourself. Take note: you are moving the questions to the past: "What do I feel?" becomes "What did I feel?" Decide for yourself whether you can use this formula in future discussions. (It's almost always possible to call a brief time out, for a coffee or to use the toilet!)

2

THREE DIMENSIONS

OF INFLUENCE

All the forms of talking to one another, of communicating with each other, have two elements in common: individuals are trying to connect with one another and, in the broadest sense of the word, people are attempting to influence each other. There are countless possible influence objectives, ranging from gaining personal acceptance, through understanding something, to taking specific action.

There is also virtually no limit to the forms which this influence behaviour can take, including non-verbal forms such as writing proposals, showing graphics, nodding or shaking the head, demonstrating something; but in most cases verbal communications remains the most important. This is because only face-to-face verbal communication can result in the need for connection being truly met.

It is useful to have a simple model of verbal influence behaviour which is easy to understand and remember, yet broad enough to allow for the full richness of all verbal behaviours to be covered. In this chapter we elaborate on such a model. This model defines influence behaviour in terms of three dimensions, which we call the *I-dimension*, the *You-dimension* and the *We-dimension*.

The value and limitations of a model

A "model" is a representation of a specific aspect of reality. Many other aspects are deliberately excluded. That one aspect is illuminated and enlarged. A model seeks to make this aspect understandable and usable. A model of influence behaviour makes it possible to "speak the same language" when talking about communicative behaviour. It makes observed behaviour easily and unambiguously nameable, using terms which are readily understood by speaker and listener. The model must permit inclusion of all possible verbal influence behaviours.

The model which we offer here is a didactic tool based on observation and experience and which has proven its value in practice over time. Though the model was designed in the first instance to describe influence behaviour in the organisational setting, we have heard many people comment that they benefited from the insights gained by working with the model and its constituent behaviours in many other settings: with life partners, children or in the context of volunteer organisations.

In the first instance, the model's value lies in the names or labels given to specific types of behaviour, and to the verbal formulations which exemplify these behaviours. It does more, however. It also makes clear that we have at our disposal a very wide range of influence behaviours, a range from which we can and must constantly make choices.

Personal responsibility

In which circumstances is it best to choose which form of behaviour? This question raises the issue of our own responsibility. People frequently speak without any particular intention; they simply say whatever comes to mind. In so doing, however, they ignore their own responsibility for the impact of their behaviour upon others. Our intention is not to help people say whatever comes to mind more eloquently. We wish to stimulate individuals to consider their intentions and the manner in which they give expression to those intentions, in as responsible a manner as possible. Underlying any effective verbal action directed towards another person there must be a clear and transparent intention and a firm commitment on the speaker's part. For example, asking an open question implies that there is a genuine interest in or curiosity about the views of another person; making a statement of purported fact implies that the speaker assumes responsibility for the truth of the statement. Speaking carries with it a responsibility; it engages the listener because it commits the speaker.

Working with the influence model helps individuals to choose their behaviours with care: with care towards oneself, with care towards the others and with care towards the objective which is being served.

A model of influence behaviour

There are many useful influence models currently in widespread use. Most use some form of metaphorical language to make it more interesting and more intuitive; for example, "parent-adult-child', or "pull and push" energies. Our influence model is based on a spatial metaphor. We have distinguished between three dimensions of behaviour; a graphical representation of the model is drawn as a three-dimensional space, with the three axes labelled *"I"*, *"You"* and *"We"*. In each dimension we have identified two to four specific component behaviours. Note that in this chapter we will describe and discuss only the verbal aspects of influence behaviour. Other equally important aspects will be dealt with in subsequent chapters.

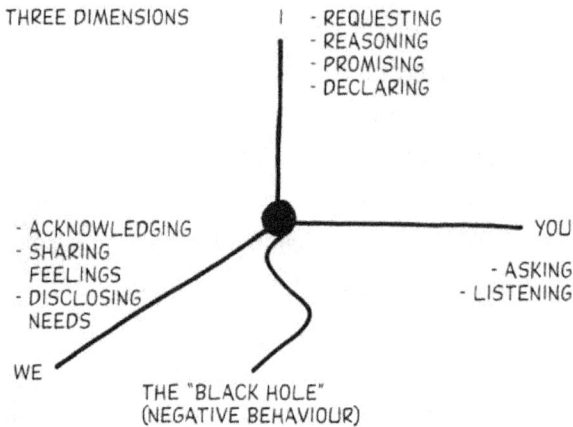

THREE DIMENSIONS · REQUESTING · REASONING · PROMISING · DECLARING

· ACKNOWLEDGING · SHARING FEELINGS · DISCLOSING NEEDS

YOU · ASKING · LISTENING

WE

THE "BLACK HOLE" (NEGATIVE BEHAVIOUR)

We consider the behaviours in the three dimensions to be of equal importance, and equally effective if used at appropriate moments. In order to have a positive impact on others it is important to possess the flexibility which allows for an easy shift from one dimension to another, as a situation unfolds. It is also important to remember that there cannot be a positive impact if there is no connection, and making the connection with another person is also a matter of finding the right language.

In order to influence others it is important to be able to move into each dimension, alone or in combinations, as the situation unfolds.

- *I-dimension*: you need the courage to take to the stage, as it were, to be seen and heard.
- *You-dimension*: you need the courage to hand the stage over to the other person, without being afraid of losing your own position. You need to be sincere when inviting the other to take the stage, to be genuinely interested in his or her view and opinions, in the confidence that it will contribute to a better, shared end-result.
- *We-dimension*: you need the courage to share the stage, to be open, and to create a mutual sense of trust and connection.

To use another metaphor: in the *I-dimension* you urge another person to see the world through your own eyes, in the *You-dimension* you try to see the world through another's eyes, and in the *We-dimension* two persons look deeply into each others' eyes.

Each dimension can be associated with a commitment and a specific type of responsibility. In order to be truly effective it is necessary to assume the associated responsibility for the commitment made consciously and deliberately:

- *I-dimension*: what I say is true, appropriate and correct. I stand by what I say. My commitment is one of responsibility for what I say.
- *You-dimension*: I take what you have to say seriously; I do my best to understand you and am open to having what you say reflect in what I think and feel. My commitment is one of responsiveness – or *response-ability* – to you and what you choose to tell me, or share with me.
- *We-dimension*: I drop my mask, and trust that you will not seek to hurt me. I stand beside you and I will not hurt you.

My commitment is one of relationship and connection: I commit myself to the development and maintenance of a positive (working) relationship with you.

In the rest of this chapter you can read what the behaviours in each dimension look like, and what sorts of impact each can have. Each dimension will be dealt with extensively.

2.1 The *I-dimension*

We begin with a sample dialogue. Jane is trying to influence Roger to undertake some important new work, using primarily the *I-dimension*. The terms used to label Jane's behaviours are noted in the dialogue and will be described further below. The dialogue is intended to provide an initial sense for the "feel" of the *I-dimension*.

Jane: (*walking into Roger's workspace...*) Hi Roger. I need to talk with you for a few minutes. [requesting]

Roger: Okay... I'm pretty busy, but go ahead.

Jane: I want you to take on designing the overall architecture for the new Zymar project. [requesting]

Roger: I don't think I can do that, Jane. I'm fully booked and deadlines are threatening on a couple of projects I'm responsible for as it is.

Jane: I know you're busy, but I'm asking you for two reasons. First, your experience makes you an obvious choice for this job. Secondly, the Zymar project could prove to be the most important new development in our department for years, certainly in terms of payback. Besides, I know you love a challenge! [reasoning]

Roger: Yes, well, but...

Jane: Roger, sometimes we all need to look beyond the boundaries of our own roles and consider the greater context – and what is best for the company! [declaring]

Roger: You're right I guess, but that doesn't help me to deal with the pressures and deadlines I have to cope with right now.

Jane: What I have always admired about you is your great sense of responsibility. I've got to give you that! [declaring]

Roger: Well, thanks...

Jane: Roger, I want you to agree to take this on. If you do that then I will work with you to convince our manager to give some of your current work to Bernard. He has been working with you for a year now, and should be quite capable of taking on more responsibility. [requesting, promising]

Roger: You've almost got me, Jane. Give me an hour to think about it and I'll get back to you by four o'clock.

Jane: Okay, you've got it. Remember, though: I'm counting on you! [declaring]

A person behaving or "acting" in the *I-dimension* makes his/her presence felt. The person becomes visible and audible, and demands to be heard. The individual empowers him – or herself, requests an audience, and asks that the listener hear what is said and to take it seriously. This is possible because he/she stands by what is said, commits him – or herself to the statements, and takes responsibility for them. The speaker's commitment is, in effect, that what is said is true or appropriate, and that the listener can count on the speaker's integrity and honesty. Of course, the *I-dimension* can be used successfully only if the speaker is sure of what he wants and knows. The importance of the *I-dimension* for increasing one's influence is evident: if well spoken and based on a relationship of mutual trust[11] the listener will respond by acting in accordance with the speaker's intent.

Within the *I-dimension* we distinguish between four types or categories of behaviour: *Requesting, Reasoning, Promising* and *Declaring*.

Requesting

Examples:[12]

- Let's think this over for a day or so before making a decision.
- I'd appreciate your undivided attention for ten minutes while I try to explain my position.
- Please do not discuss this matter with anyone outside this room.
- I suggest we analyse the data before discussing strategy.
- Here's my proposal: We launch a pilot programme in Frank's region and then, if successful, roll it out nationwide.
- What are the latest sales projections for the northern region?

---

[11]See Chapter 3 for more on the importance of trust.

[12]The examples given are all drawn from the organisational context. Similar lists of examples could easily be drawn from family and social contexts, or from exchanges as they occur in volunteer organisations.

- I must insist that you complete your part of the report by Friday!
- I'd like you to think about my suggestion and come back to me by the end of the week with a final project plan.

When Requesting we seek to gain the listener(s) agreement to *do* or *not to do* something. The speaker may formulate his action as a hint, a suggestion, a proposal, demand or indeed a command. The formulation chosen depends on the pressure, which the speaker wishes to exert.

Check out your own level of comfort in and facility with Requesting:

Do you

- Make regular suggestions about how to move things forward?.
- Express your proposals and suggestions with conviction?
- Seek necessary information in a clear and unambiguous manner?
- Emphasise proposals or requests with appropriate non-verbal behaviour (eye-contact, voice, posture, gestures)?
- State directly what you expect of others?
- Present your suggestions or proposals concisely and clearly?

How would other people respond to these questions with regard to your behaviour?

Reasoning

Examples:

- Recent studies have shown that Chinese consumer electronics producers are more innovative than their competitors in the West.
- There are no tickets available for tonight's concert.
- Three clinical tests have shown that zenobarbitol is the most effective drug for combating hysterical dementia.
- I have two major reasons for not agreeing with your proposal: first...; and second....
- My experience of the Indian culture has convinced me that the best way to present our products successfully there is to...
- If we agree about this, then cutting back on production is the logical next step.

When Reasoning, the speaker is basing him- or herself on facts, logic and experience. The speaker is committing to and seeking the listener's acceptance of and agreement with the truth of what is said, and takes responsibility for the truth of statements made or the accuracy and relevance of the arguments presented. These arguments are intended to lead the other person to an inescapable conclusion: "You are right", "That is indeed the way it is", "This solution is not going to work". Though Reasoning usually appeals explicitly to relevant facts and the logical steps taken in thinking something through, these may only be implied. If so requested, the speaker implies that she or he *could* back up the statements with facts, data, and analyses. The speaker advocates a certain position, decision, or solution by arguing in its favour, or argues against a position, decision or solution advocated by the other person – always on the basis of facts and reasons as they are available at the time.

Using Reasoning implies that the speaker stands behind the accuracy and relevance of the presented statements or arguments. It also implies that the speaker is open to the facts and reasoning of the other person: a position held may be modified or abandoned if the other party can provide convincing contrary evidence. The speaker does not cling to a position because of personal values, beliefs or convictions, but only because the evidence, as currently available, supports it. The expression, "My mind is made up; don't bother me with the facts!", usually voiced in a tongue-in-cheek manner, suggests that facts and logic were not the primary determinants of the position being held at all, and is therefore an expression suggestive of Declaring rather than of Reasoning.

Of all the behaviours within the *I-dimension*, Reasoning is the least personal, in that the speaker reveals less of him or herself than is the case with the other three behaviours. The focus is on facts and logic, not on persons or personalities. Pure Reasoning leaves no room for emotion. In today's organisations, Reasoning is frequently backed up by PowerPoint presentations; the focus of the listener's attention is on the data being presented rather than on the presenter.

Check out your own level of comfort in and facility with Reasoning:

Do you

- Draw conclusions from facts and arguments in a persuasive fashion?
- Base your assertions and arguments on verifiable facts and logic?
- Argue for or against positions in a clear and structured manner?
- Maintain a calm and rational composure during discussions?
- Present arguments clearly and concisely?
- Express views and opinions clearly even when others disagree?

How would other people respond to these questions with regard to your behaviour?

Promising

Examples:

- I promise to give you my response via email by 5 o'clock.
- I will not discuss this matter with anyone without clearing it first with you.
- I give you my word; I'll be there at eight.
- You can count on my complete support for the strategy you have just outlined.
- I will attend this afternoon's meeting *or* I will complete the documentation you requested; I will not do both.
- No. I am not going to do that.
- My commitment to this project is for two days a week, no more.

When Promising, the speaker is committing himself to undertake a specific action within a specific timeframe. Equally important: the speaker makes clear what he or she is *not* prepared to undertake. For many individuals, saying "no" is extremely difficult: the result is over-commitment and not being able to follow through on commitments made. "Promising" requires that the speaker be very clear on what he or she is and is not able and willing to do, and implies an unambiguous commitment to follow through.

Promising responsibly and with integrity is a result of the underlying intention, and that intention is not to get rid of the person making a request, but to be honest and transparent – even when that means saying "no" clearly. It happens too often that, at the end of a conversation or meeting, it remains unclear who is going to do what. Both – or all – parties need to clear.

Check out your own levels of comfort in and facility with Promising

Do you
- When promising to do something, do so convincingly?
- Offer help readily?
- Agree to specific time frames and conditions?
- Follow through reliably on commitments made?
- Say "no" clearly when you are unwilling or unable to comply with someone else's request?
- Use non-verbal behaviour (tone of voice, eye-contact and gestures) in a manner which creates trust when promising to do something?

How would other people respond to these questions with regard to your behaviour?

Declaring

Examples:

- That was an extremely valuable comment you made this morning!
- I really like the way you handled that situation!
- Your tactics have not been fair!
- I didn't like the way you spoke about your colleagues just then!
- We must never, ever forget that in this organisation we treat individuals with respect at all times!
- We are *all* responsible for customer satisfaction!

By using Declaring, norms and values or value judgments are made explicit. One can express a judgment of something the listener has said or done, or take a stand on an issue, based on personal values. There is often an exclamation mark at the end of the sentence.

There is no *logic* involved. What is said is a declaration based on personal values and norms. Such a declaration may be seen as a fact and presented as a fact, but it only *becomes* a fact by being said. Declaring does not necessarily refer to the past. The speaker may state what he believes he and others *should* be striving for. Articulating a vision of a possible and desirable future, articulating a "mission statement", seeking to inspire listeners to follow the speaker on a certain course; all are various forms of Declaring.

Check out your own levels of comfort in and facility with Declaring

Do you

- Make unambiguous evaluative statements (good/bad, fair/unfair, etc.)?
- Give direct and honest feedback?
- Challenge the appropriateness of a suggested course of action if it is inconsistent with your own values?
- Make clear which personal convictions and values guide your behaviour?
- Let others know on which fundamental values your actions are based?
- Use appropriate non-verbal behaviour to emphasise your statements?

How would other people respond to these questions with regard to your behaviour?

Criteria for effectiveness: the I-dimension

When an individual stands up to be heard, it is the intention that, at the very least, the listener *understands*. Understanding is made much easier if the speaker adheres to a few simple guidelines: 'simple' in theory, but certainly not always so in practice.

I-dimension statements are more easily understood if:

- they are concise;
- they are concrete, precise and specific;
- there is a transparent structure in their presentation;
- statements are labelled appropriately (e.g. "I'd like to make a proposal at this point" or "Okay, here is what I'm prepared to do for you");

- the other person experiences an appropriate amount of pressure;
- tone of voice, facial expression and gestures are congruent with the spoken message.

Sometimes people fear that effective or strong use of the *I-dimension* will simply result in an argument (or worse). This concern is understandable, because the *I-dimension* involves applying pressure and if one is not used to doing so it will feel uncomfortable. *I-dimension* behaviour can be experienced by a listener as being quite forceful, and the amount of pressure which is appropriate depends on the situation. The *I-dimension* is not about being aggressive; it is about being assertive. "Connecting" can also take place through putting another person under appropriate pressure. A well-managed disagreement sometimes helps enormously to strengthen a relationship, at work and at home.

"I" DIMENSION

- REQUESTING, PROPOSING, DEMANDING
- REASONING, ARGUING FOR OR AGAINST
- PROMISING, SAYING NO
- DECLARING, TAKING A STAND, JUDGING

APPROPRIATE PRESSURE

CONCISE

STRUCTURE

CONCRETE

Being Concise

There is sometimes a tendency to think that the more arguments one can produce, the more solid one's position will be. This is an illusion. People cannot digest very much information, so usually they will switch off after a minute or so. If there is no attention being paid, the arguments fall on deaf ears and are a waste of energy. In addition, too many arguments give the other the chance to select the weakest argument to pick apart. If one of your arguments is weak then there will even be a tendency to think that the rest are weak as well. It is best to force yourself to stick to your strongest arguments and to keep the rest available for possible use later on. Finally, a lot of talk comes across as chatter, unbridled thinking. That does your image no good at all. Around two-thousand years ago the Greco-Roman philosopher Epictetus wrote:

> *First and foremost, think before you speak to make sure you are speaking with good purpose. Glib talk is disrespectful to others. Breezy self-disclosure is disrespectful to yourself.*
>
> *If we babble about every idea that occurs to us – big and small – we can easily fritter away, in the trivial currents of mindless talk, ideas that have true merit. Unchecked speech is like a vehicle wildly lurching out of control and destined for the ditch.*
>
> *Enter into discussions when social or professional occasion calls for it, but be cautious that the spirit and intent of the discussion and its content remain worthy. Prattle is seductive. Stay out of its clutches.*[13]

---

[13]Epictetus: *Manual for Living*. Interpretation by Sharon Lebell.1994: 62-63

Silence

Words stand out best if they are framed in silence. Silence can be a strong medium of communication, and can express a great deal, such as attention, concentration, respect and seriousness. In some cultures silence is particularly valued, for example among the Lakota, a Native American people:

> *Silence was meaningful with the Lakota, and granting a space of silence before talking was done in the practice of true politeness and regardful of the rule that "thought comes before speech." Silence was a mark of respect. More powerful than words was silence with the Lakota. Silence meant to the Lakota what it meant to Disraeli when he said, "Silence is the mother of truth", for the silent man was ever to be trusted, while the man ever ready with speech was never taken seriously.*[14]

2.2 The *You-dimension*

We begin again with a sample dialogue. Jane hopes to influence Roger to undertake some additional work, and she uses primarily the *You-dimension*.

Jane: Hi Roger! You look very busy. Is it convenient for you to give me a few minutes now or later? [asking]

Roger: You're right about "busy", but sure, go ahead. What's up?

Jane: You know about the Zymar project of course, and at the last meeting you commented on the challenges

---

[14]Chief Luther Standing Bear, in *Native American Wisdom*, compiled by Kent Nerburn and Louise Mengelkoch. 1991: 8.

we'd have to face in tackling it. Can you tell me some more about what you were thinking of when you said that? [asking]

Roger: Yeah, well, I was of course thinking primarily in terms of the software requirements. From an architectural point of view it is really going to take us into unknown territory.

Jane: I understand that you mean that there may not be many people around who can confront the challenges adequately. [listening]

Roger: That's right, I don't.

Jane: Tell me if I'm wrong, but I thought I caught a sort a glint in your eye when you talked about "unknown territory"! [listening]

Roger: Yes, well it would certainly be challenging, and I'd like that, if only...

Jane: "If only" what? [asking]

Roger: Well, I feel swamped right now, and a couple of crucial deadlines are looming.

Jane: I get the impression that you'd really like to take on the Zymar project, *if only* someone else could take over some of your current work. [listening]

Roger: Yes, I think you're right!

Jane: Can you see a way to make that happen? [asking]

Roger: Well, I could try to get some of the work I am currently responsible for moved to Bernard, but I would need to convince the other project sponsors.

Jane: You think this would be possible? [asking]

Roger: Well, maybe ...

Roles are reversed when entering the *You-dimension*. It's not the initiator, with his or her views and opinions, who is the focus of attention, but the other person. The *You-dimension* is not just about letting someone else have his or her say; it is about actively seeking to understand what someone means or how someone else experiences a situation. It is driven by sincere interest. It involves a commitment to take what the speaker is trying to convey seriously and to respond accordingly. It signals a willingness to let the other's words sink in, to take the other's message on board and to let it impact on the listener's own subsequent thinking and behaviour. This is not, of course, the equivalent to agreeing with everything the speaker says.

The importance of the *You-dimension* has been expressed as follows: "Seek first to understand, and then to be understood."[15] If a person wishes that his or her suggestions, ideas and arguments have positive impact, then that person needs to understand where the other person is coming from. In addition, of course, it may result in learning something from the experience of others, aspects of an issue which may have been missed.

The *You-dimension* includes two specific behaviours: *Asking* and *Listening*.

Asking

Examples:

* What do you believe the best course of action would be?
* How do you feel about what you have heard so far?

---

[15] Stephen R. Covey: The 7 *Habits of Highly Effective People*, 1990: 237

- Please help me to understand why you feel so strongly about this.
- You mentioned "cynicism"; could you say more about that?
- You voiced your concern that... Earlier you said you believed that... I'm not sure I understand the link. Could you say some more about that?

Through Asking, the other person is *invited* to share his or her experience, vision, ideas, hopes or understanding. Follow-through questions can be used to seek deeper understanding. It is risky to think too quickly, "OK, I've understood". The *You-dimension* is not about seeking confirmation for what one already thinks or knows, but about trying to find out how it is that another person might look at a situation differently.

Sometimes people confuse Asking with simply asking a lot of questions. Though many questions do belong within the realm of the *You-dimension*, many others do not: interrogative questions, interview questions, leading questions or purely informational questions with no purpose other than to complement one's own understanding of a situation. These types of questions belong in the *I-dimension*, and usually in the category Requesting (information). The *You-dimension* is about understanding how another person sees, feels about or experiences situations; it is not just about learning the facts of a situation or satisfying one's own curiosity. The speaker's "agenda", what he or she wishes to explain or talk about, is central and the listener does not try to influence it (*I-dimension* behaviour). The listener may, of course, choose to enquire about that agenda: "Help me to understand why you are continuing with this and not that line of thought." Open questions are usually more effective than closed questions. "Why" questions need to be used with caution. Think of who, in early years, asked questions like: "Why haven't you finished your homework?" "Why haven't you tidied your room?" Why questions are often experienced as a demand for justification.

Check out your own levels of comfort in and facility with Asking:

Do you
- Enquire after the views and opinions of others?
- Convey a sincere interest in the other?
- Seek honest personal feedback?
- Use follow-through questions to get to the heart of what someone is trying to express or explain?
- Invite others to share their feelings?
- Indicate your interest by means of your voice, posture and gestures when you enquire?

How would other people respond to these questions with regard to your behaviour?

Listening

Examples:
- So your idea is that we should first...
- Let me see if I have understood: your main concern is...
- I get the impression that you are quite discouraged by recent events.
- Okay. It sounds as if you have two significant reservations about this plan. First... and second... Right?

• If you had more staff your problems would be over. Is that what you're telling me?

Being a listener means ceasing to speak what comes into one's own mind and letting someone else speak what is on his or her mind. Listening means "Active Listening": being present with full attention, with verbal and non-verbal signals, which indicate listening. It involves testing one's understanding by paraphrasing, summarising or reflecting back what one thinks the other person meant or intended, not only at the level of stated words but also at the level of (often) unstated feelings. It does not mean repeating back the words which the speaker used (also called "parroting"); it involves trying to capture the essence of the speaker's message in one's own words, sometimes by just repeating back a single key word. Listening is more than using one's ears and keeping one's mouth shut. When someone says "I hear you," it generally means he has stopped listening.

Listening is about listening to what the *other* person is saying and trying to extract his or her meaning; it is not about listening to one's own reactions or thoughts as these are triggered by the words of the other person. Effective listening requires that one "park" one's own thoughts, follow the speaker without overtaking; and yield right-of-way to the speaker if her words start to get entangled with the listener's own thoughts.

It is generally accepted that 80% of human communication takes place at the non-verbal level. Listening effectively implies trying to tune into and understand that which is being communicated at the non-verbal level as well as at the spoken level.

Check out your own levels of comfort in and facility with Listening:

Do you

- Test your understanding by regularly summarising what others have said?
- Use appropriate non-verbal behaviour (e.g. eye-contact, nodding, open posture) when listening?
- Permit silence to give the speaker time to think?
- Listen effectively in situations marked by disagreement or conflict?
- "Listen" to non-verbal behaviour (expression, gestures, tone of voice) to pick up on unstated feelings?
- Remain calm and patient when others are speaking?

How would other people respond to these questions with regard to your behaviour?

Criteria for Effectiveness: The You-dimension

The *You-dimension* requires that the listener:

- be genuinely interested in the views of the other
- take sufficient time to seek true understanding
- follow the line of thought of the other person
- place his/her own thoughts and objectives in parentheses, in the knowledge that they can be returned to, in time.

Sometimes individuals express a concern that they might lose their own influence by granting the other person so much attention and space. They are afraid of becoming too receptive to the views of the other person and having to change their own views. That danger is indeed present! One's own views *might* change as the result of gaining a better and broader understanding. On the other hand, the listener will be in a better position to act in the *You-dimension* if he or she has sufficient confidence in the ability to return to personal views at the appropriate moment. That confidence confers the ability to focus entirely and calmly on the other person.

The *You-dimension* makes every interaction more complex: the listener gets drawn into the world of another person. The listener has the courage to not only put aside his or her own views and opinions but also, possibly, to change them. The *You-dimension* is sometimes seen as purely tactical: only by understanding another person fully is it possible, after all, to effectively convey one's own thoughts and feelings in a manner which exerts influence. The *You-dimension* implies more, however. It implies a willingness to sharpen, change and even to let go of one's own, perhaps cherished, views and beliefs. When the required courage is lacking, the result, too often, is discussions and meetings during which a great deal is transmitted but very little truly received.

There is of course more that happens when Asking and Listening authentically. Not only might the listener's thoughts be impacted, the process of Asking and Listening frequently triggers an entire new line of thought in the other person. This is of course the essence of effective coaching.

To listen closely and reply well is the highest perfection we are able to attain in the art of conversation.
François de La Rochefoucauld

"YOU" DIMENSION

- ASKING, INVITING
- LISTENING ACTIVELY, ALLOWING SILENCE, PARAPHRASING

THROUGH
OTHER'S EYES

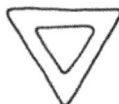

YIELD RIGHT OF WAY
TO OTHER

THE OTHER DETERMINES
DIRECTION AND SPEED

PARK OWN OBJECTIVES,
IDEAS, SOLUTIONS

Effective use of the You-dimension requires that:

- you show interest and curiosity, learn to see the world through the other's eyes;
- the other always has right of way in terms of what he or she wishes to talk about;
- the other determines his or her own tempo and the direction of the conversation;
- you let go for the time being of your own objectives, views and opinions, and (brilliant) solutions and answers.

2.3 The *We-dimension*

We begin once again with a sample dialogue. Jane is trying to influence Roger to undertake some additional work, this time using primarily the *We-dimension*. The terms used to label Jane's behaviours are described below.

Jane: Hey, Roger. I've been looking at the Zymar project with an eye to getting it up and running, but I'm worried about some issues. [sharing feelings]

Roger: It's going to be challenging for sure! But what specifically is on your mind?

Jane: My concern is about the software architecture. What's required would be breaking new ground for us and I don't know if we're up to it. [disclosing needs]

Roger: Yes, that aspect had occurred to me too. Do we have the necessary skilled resources?

Jane: I can only think of one, to be honest, and that is you. So of course I thought of asking you directly, but I know how overloaded you are at the moment. If I were in your position I think I'd have to say "no" to this one. So I'm feeling sort of lost at the moment. [acknowledging, sharing feelings]

Roger: Hmmm. I wonder if...

Jane: What...?

Roger: Well, I really would like to help out and it is certainly a challenge worth taking on. I wonder if Bernard might be ready to take some of the current project work off my shoulders... You know, I think it might work, but I need to feel confident that we can convince our manager.

Jane: I feel so much better already, knowing that you are thinking along with me on this. [sharing feelings]

Roger: Let me think about it for an hour or so; I'll get back to you by four o'clock.

Jane: You're great, Roger! Thanks so very much! [sharing feelings] Is there anything I can do to help?

Roger: Let me think first...

When in the *I-dimension*, I want you to understand me. When in the *You-dimension* I want to understand you. When in the *We-dimension* I seek to build a bridge across our separateness and seek to create a true connection, so that we can move forward together. "It takes two to tango." "Two heads are better than one." Everyday expressions like these demonstrate a general acknowledgment of the fact that very little of true significance can be accomplished alone. In order to work together it is essential that the parties involved trust each other implicitly, respect each other and feel connected with one another.

If we apply the metaphor of the stage, you could say that though there are successful one-man shows and monologues, most interesting theatre requires more actors on stage. There has to be a chemistry between the actors, and between actors and public, to create intriguing and exciting theatre. The players have to trust and value each other, and be on the same wavelength. The same is true of colleagues working together on a project.

Mutual trust and a healthy (working) relationship do not come automatically. The *We-dimension* describes three specific behaviours which are central to building trust and developing that healthy relationship: Acknowledging, Sharing Feelings and Disclosing Needs. Using them demonstrates a preparedness to invest in the relationship in an open manner and with integrity. Something develops which is central to every person in (work) life: a sense of being seen, heard and acknowledged as a person.

Acknowledging

Examples:

- If I were in your position then I would also be concerned about...
- That must be very difficult for you.
- I can quite imagine your being upset about this.
- With the information available to you, I would probably have reached the same conclusion.
- I sense that we find our inspiration in the same sources.
- Given your role I can understand that you want to steer that course.

In order to develop an effective working relationship the partners need to dare to establish real contact. Listening, even active listening is not enough. It also requires the ability to put oneself in the other's place, to give verbal expression to one's understanding of how things might look and feel to the other person. The term *empathy* is usually used to designate this ability.

Showing empathy acknowledges the other person. It sends a clear message to the other which says "I accept and value you. How you think about things, experience things and feel about things is important to me." It includes sincere expressions of respect and regard for the other's knowledge, experience and expertise, even in the face of possible disagreement. It is also powerfully conveyed through non-verbal behaviour like posture, facial expression and eye-contact (in Western culture at least).

Check out your own levels of comfort in and facility with Acknowledging:

Do you

- Acknowledge others' experience, expertise or achievements openly?
- Show that you can also see issues from others' points of view?
- Show respect for the legitimacy of others' points of view even when in disagreement?
- Demonstrate empathic understanding of others' concerns or feelings?
- Take others and their views seriously?
- Underline your acceptance and valuing of the other person with appropriate non-verbal signals?

How would other people respond to these questions with regard to your behaviour?

Sharing Feelings

Examples:

- I'm feeling very uncertain about my ability to contribute in a meaningful way here.
- I am delighted by the progress we have made on this!
- The current forecast upsets me deeply.
- I am really excited about the possibility of...
- That's a terrific achievement, I feel like celebrating!

We expect of others that they be open with us, but they are often only prepared to be open when they have first seen openness on our part. It requires courage to drop the masks behind which we so readily hide, being candid about feelings, both positive and negative. That is not always easy to do.

Sharing Feelings with integrity involves *owning* the feelings. We are often quick to externalise feelings, as if they are something done to us by others. Perhaps what someone else said or did was a "trigger" but we are always responsible for our own feelings. Sharing Feelings requires us to recognise and acknowledge our feelings as our own, and this requires the ability to reflect, to get in touch with oneself. When we blame others for our feelings, we slip into the category Declaring in the *I-dimension*.

An example might help to clarify this. Imagine someone making each of the following statements. To which behaviour category does each belong?

1. I am feeling really irritated about a few things my boss said this morning.
2. My boss can be pretty irritating sometimes.
3. When you said that, I felt very irritated.
4. That was a very irritating comment you made.
5. You are a very irritating person!

Though so very much depends on the non-verbal behaviour accompanying each statement, statements 1 and 3 would normally fall under the category Sharing Feelings, while statements 2 and 4, which are evaluative judgments, fall under the category Declaring. Statement 5, particularly when said in a critical and aggressive manner, is very negative and potentially destructive. It amounts to a rejection of the other person, and therefore falls into the category of "negative behaviours". (See 2.4 below).

Check out your own levels of comfort in and facility with Sharing Feelings:

Do you

- Acknowledge own uncertainty and confusion?
- Express warmth or affection openly?
- Let others know *in a non-judgemental manner* when their actions have stirred negative or positive feelings?
- Confide your hopes and dreams to others?
- Share feelings of joy or happiness, sorrow or sadness?
- Let others know what is personally important to you by being transparent about your feelings?

How would other people respond to these questions with regard to your behaviour?

Disclosing Needs

Examples:

- I am going to need help in order to...
- I'm stuck, and need further insight into...
- What's really at stake here for me is....
- To be honest, I need recognition for my contribution to...
- A dream which I've never been able to realise is...
- When working in a team what's important to me is...

Behind feelings lie needs which are either being met (leading to positive feelings) or not being met (leading to negative feelings).[16] A second aspect of being open lies in disclosing

---

[16]Marshall B. Rosenberg, *Nonviolent Communication*. 2000.

needs, what one needs in order to flourish. When disclosing needs, one makes oneself vulnerable to a certain degree. In effect one says, "I can't do this alone. I need help with this." Acknowledging a need for help, to the right person at the right time, is a sign of wisdom, not weakness. It may require courage to acknowledge needs. Unlike with Requesting, however, there is no direct or explicit expectation that the listener respond to the disclosure with anything other than understanding.

Check out your own levels of comfort in and facility with Disclosing Needs:
Do you
- Let others know when you need help or assistance?
- Admit to your own shortcomings or weaknesses?
- Tell others what your underlying motivation is?
- Disclose unfulfilled or unrealised ambitions or dreams?
- Let others know when you need some personal "space" or time to think?
- Candidly express your needs for recognition, encouragement etc.?

How would other people respond to these questions with regard to your behaviour?

Further Reflections on the We-dimension

Use of the *We-dimension* behaviours will quickly reveal their importance in terms of building trust and establishing connection. We pay particular attention to this Dimension because, in our experience, its importance is frequently underestimated. Many training programmes focus on *I-dimension* behaviours (presentation skills) or the *You-dimension* (the art of asking questions). Without openness and trust business discussions frequently develop into a more or less civilised version of trench warfare.

People sometimes wonder whether the use of the behaviours in this dimension to "drop the mask", is possible in a work environment. They wonder whether such behaviours belong more appropriately in their personal lives. On the contrary: personal feelings largely determine whether the climate and the culture of the work environment are productive or diseased!

There is sometimes also a concern that the openness and vulnerability which accompany the *We-dimension* might be misused. That danger is undeniably present. Nevertheless, the benefits far outweigh the possible risks: everybody does, in the end, wish to be seen, heard and valued as an individual. Where a climate of openness and mutual trust can be established much more can be achieved than might be expected.

Finally: *a sorrow shared is a sorrow halved.* By sharing your feelings their pressure on your mood usually becomes less. They become a subject of discussion and do not stand as a barrier between you and the other. You remain responsible for your own feelings, but the empathy of the other can make them much more bearable.

"WE" DIMENSION
- ACKNOWLEDGING/EMPATHISING
  WITH OTHER'S FEELINGS & NEEDS
- SHARING OWN FEELINGS
- DISCLOSING NEEDS

OPENNESS STIMULATES OPENNESS
TRUSTING CREATES TRUST
OPENNESS AND TRUST LEAD TO
STRONG (WORKING) RELATIONSHIPS

2.4 Negative Behaviours

Our influence model seeks to describe positive behaviours. All those behaviours, if used appropriately, can be highly effective. Implicit in the thinking behind the model is also the high value placed on authenticity and integrity.

Not *all* behaviours, however, fit into the model; some types of behaviour are inherently ineffective, negative or destructive. They deny or avoid responsibility and undermine trust and relationship. They are defensive in nature. Putting oneself or another down, sends a message that influencing is an impossible venture. It creates a climate of mistrust and hopelessness.

We describe this type of behaviour in order to make it easier to recognise it and, if necessary, to be able to name it when holding up the mirror to someone – or to oneself!

Forms of negative behaviour include cynicism, sarcasm, trivialising, discouraging, and criticising. There is nothing wrong with being critical, except when there is a constant negative undertone. Criticising others and their ideas, putting down one's own organisation, belittling oneself or being sarcastic are behaviours which suck away warmth and positive energy, making it disappear into a sort of black hole. An image which comes to mind is that of the "Dementors" in the *Harry Potter* novels. When they approach everything turns dark and cold. Some forms of so-called humour can have the same effect.

By Discouraging, we mean placing a kind of wet blanket on others and their hopes or ideas. While it is useful to dampen totally unrealistic ambitions, dreams or ideas, it is stifling to personal energy and enthusiasm to have to face a barrage of comments which declare those ambitions or dreams or ideas to be no more than naïve fantasy. Trivialising, is a manner of putting down oneself or others with comments intended to make the extraordinary seem ordinary; the valuable, insignificant; or the outstanding, commonplace.

For a fourth time we offer a sample dialogue. Jane seems to be attempting to influence Roger to undertake some additional work, but she slips into a great deal of negative behaviour.

Jane: Hi Roger, you probably don't have any time, as usual, but there is something I'd like to discuss with you.

Roger: Oh? What's that?

Jane: Well, it's probably a waste of time. It's about the Zymar project, but I think it's about to be still-born.

Roger: Why do you say that?

Jane: Basically I just don't think this organisation is

anywhere near being able to cope with the challenges involved.

Roger: Sorry to hear you say that, Jane! Frankly, though it would make us break new ground, I think we can give it a really good shot.

Jane: Mr. Optimism as always! Easy for you to say because you don't have the time get involved anyway, squirreled away as you are with your own little projects.

Roger: Well, there might be a way...

Jane: No, just forget I ever raised the issue. I think I'll just tell our manager to scrub the whole plan. He'll probably throw a fit, but what else is new?

Roger (as Jane walks away, and not intending to be heard): Have a nice day, Miss Sunshine.

Negative behaviours keep others at a distance; they have an implosive effect on the environment in which individuals are trying to communicate – and influence each other. It is generally not true of course that (as in the example above!) whole conversations are dominated exclusively by negative behaviours. Usually it is a case of the occasional negative note destroying the impact of other possibly very positive and sincere contributions.

Further examples:
- We'll never get it right; we might as well give up now.
- She never listens to anyone except herself; just like a broken record.
- That will never work in this organisation.
- It's no big deal; anyone could have done it.

- Dream on!
- I'm such an idiot!
- I've met a dog with more insight than you!

Check out the extent to which you might slip into negative behaviours:

Do you
- Belittle yourself or put yourself down?
- Make jokes at the expense of others?
- Make cynical comments?
- Make strongly negative comments about people, situations or possibilities?
- Belittle the accomplishments of others?
- Fall silent and withdraw when someone challenges you?

How would other people respond to these questions with regard to your behaviour?

2.5 When to Use Which Dimension?

Though the following guidelines are not intended to be exhaustive they can help you to think about the behaviour or combination of behaviours, which would be most appropriate in any given influence situation.

The I-dimension

Use Requesting when:
- You are clear on what you want and the other party can provide it;
- It is appropriate that your standards or expectations be met;

- You have useful suggestions, which could help to achieve the goal;
- It is necessary that others take specific actions.

Use Reasoning when:
- You have facts and data, and/or reasonable hypotheses based on facts;
- You enjoy credibility in the eyes of the other;
- You have thought through your line of reasoning carefully;
- Emotions are not a dominant factor, either for you or the other person.

Use Promising when:
- You are willing to make a binding commitment;
- The other is clear on what he or she wants or expects of you;
- It is necessary that you be clear on the limits to which you are prepared to go;
- It is necessary that you take specific actions.

Use Declaring when:
- You have formed a judgment which the other person should know about;
- It is appropriate that you articulate a goal, mission or ideal;
- Others are unclear and directionless;
- You have made a clear choice in your mind.

The You-dimension

Use Asking and Listening when:
- You would benefit from understanding the other's point of view;

- You need to understand the other's mood, feelings, goals etc.;
- You do not understand the other's reasoning;
- You do not understand the other's needs or interests.

The We-dimension

Use Acknowledging when:

- It is important to build a relationship marked by mutual trust;
- The other is emotionally upset;
- It is important that the other feels accepted and respected;
- You feel and wish to convey an empathic connection with the other person.

Use Sharing Feelings and Disclosing Needs when:

- Building trust is important;
- Deep mutual understanding is important;
- You need or desire someone's help;
- You feelings or needs are very much in the foreground.

Switching Between Dimensions

Flexibility is not only a matter of using behaviours from different dimensions in different situations; it is also a matter of being able to switch from one dimension to another within a single conversation. You need to be able to do this smoothly. In order to achieve something you cannot rely on one-dimensional behaviour. You need to make combinations, as in the example below:

Why?	Movement	Example	Behaviours
To see whether your proposal has gone down well.	*I-dimension* → *You-dimension*	My proposal is that we go with this supplier. What are your thoughts on this?	Proposing → Asking
To remain in discussion in a cooperative, positive manner.	*I-dimension* → *We-dimension*	That's just what I am not prepared to do. But I can imagine that you find that disappointing.	Promising → Acknowledging
To stay connected with what the other has just brought in, even when disagreeing.	*You-dimension* → *I-dimension*	From what you have said it sounds like it's not going to move forward any time soon. I'd like to offer the following opposite view.	Listening → Reasoning
To show how the other's input affects you.	*You-dimension* → *We-dimension*	So you're prepared to withdraw our proposal. I now feel very disappointed.	Listening → Sharing Feelings
To supplement your need with a proposal.	*We-dimension* → *I-dimension*	I would love to see my efforts rewarded. That's why I would like you to reserve a half hour for a project evaluation at tomorrow's meeting.	Disclosing Needs → Requesting
To check whether your interpretation is correct.	*We-dimension* → *You-dimension*	I get a sense that you're really delighted with it. How *do* you feel, in your own words?	Acknowledging → Asking

Managing Irritation[17]

It is inevitable in a high-pressure work environment that individuals will irritate each other from time to time. How we *deal* with the irritating behaviour of others is critical.

Something occurs, and we make comments like:

- Don't you *ever* listen?!
- Your problem is, you're just *lazy*! (or *slow*, or *stupid*, or *unreliable* or any other negative attribute which seems applicable)
- Can you say something *constructive* for a change? (or *sensible*, or *useful*, or *positive* or whatever else)
- Well, don't get angry with *me*!

Or perhaps we don't say anything at all. We *think* these things but keep our mouths shut. Or maybe we're not even aware of *thinking* them; we just roll our eyes and try to ignore the irritant. Whatever the case, someone has done something which irritates, and we judge the behaviour negatively. How can you deal with the situation constructively? It is possible with a five-step response in which the *We-dimension* and the *I-dimension* are used in turn.

1. Stating your observation (*I-dimension*, reasoning)
2. Expressing your feelings (*We-dimension*, sharing feelings)
3. Disclosing your needs (*We-dimension*, disclosing needs)
4. Making a request (*I-dimension*, requesting)
5. Offering an exchange (*I-dimension*, promising)

---

[17]Adapted from Marshall B. Rosenberg: *Nonviolent Communication*, 2000.

We'll follow a simple example. You are trying to make an important point to someone in the course of a discussion. The other person is "obviously" not listening to you; you can tell because he interrupts, looks away when you talk and keeps coming back to his own arguments. You notice yourself getting frustrated and eventually you feel like you are about to say something like "Don't you ever listen?" or "This is useless. I feel like I'm talking to a wall!"

Observation

The first step is to pay attention only to what you have observed, and to state that in a way which is free of judgment or criticism. For example:

"John, you have interrupted me three times in the last few minutes, and I see you looking away when I'm trying to present my arguments."

"Clean" observations avoid:

- generalizing – "You're a poor listener."
- predicting – "You'll never understand what I'm trying to say."
- using evaluative adverbs or adjectives – "You're very talkative."
- inferences about the other person's thoughts, intentions or feelings – "You don't want to hear what I have to say."
- unspecific comments – "Typical marketing; you think you have all the answers!"

Feelings

An expression of personal feeling conveys information, once again without attacking the other person. In the example it might sound like:

"John, you have interrupted me three times in the last few minutes, and I see you looking away when I'm trying to present my arguments [Observation]. I am feeling frustrated and disappointed."

Expressions of feeling are *never* formulated in terms like "I feel that…". In this phrase "feel" becomes a synonym for "think". Expressions of feeling do not involve self-assessment: "I feel inadequate." Expressions of feeling do not imply an evaluation of the other person: "I feel unvalued."

In general we could say that we experience positive feelings when our needs are being met, and negative feelings when our needs are not being met. As we are generally not brought up to express feelings, our feelings vocabulary tends to be limited.

Needs
What others say and do may be the *stimulus*, but never the *cause* of our feelings. Our feelings result from how we *choose* to receive what others say and do, as well as our particular needs and expectations in that moment. Negative feelings are stimulated when our needs or not being met.

We must accept responsibility for our own feelings rather than blame other people. We can do this by acknowledging our own needs, desires, expectations, values or thoughts.

Going back to the example above, the need could be formulated as follows:

"John, you have interrupted me three times in the last few minutes, and I see you looking away when I'm trying to present my arguments [Observation]. I am feeling frustrated and disappointed [Feeling]. I need to know that we understand each other and I need your support on this project."

Request
When our needs are not being met, we follow the expression of what we are observing, feeling and needing with a specific request: we ask for actions that might ensure that our needs are met.

Requests need to be formulated positively: requesting is about what you want someone to *do*, not to *stop doing* – because such a negative request always implies criticism ("Please stop interrupting me!"). It is also important to avoid vague, abstract or ambiguous phrases ("I would like you to start showing me a little respect!"). It is important to formulate requests in the form of concrete actions that others can undertake.

If a request is formulated in such a way that it can be interpreted as a demand then resistance is likely. The difference lies in what the speaker does if the request is not complied with. It's a demand if the speaker criticises or judges if the request is not met, or if he lays on a "guilt trip". ("You'd do as I ask if you really love me!")

In the example, it could sound as follows:

"John, you have interrupted me three times in the last few minutes, and I see you looking away when I'm trying to present my arguments [Observation]. I am feeling frustrated and disappointed [Feeling]. I need to know that we understand each other and I need your support on this project [Need]. I would like you to listen to my proposal and my reasoning."

Exchange

We are perfectly entitled to request almost anything of people, as long as we are prepared to offer something in exchange – something which will meet the needs of the other party. If we don't understand the needs of the other party, then we have to ask. Once we understand, we can offer an exchange:

"John, you have interrupted me three times in the last few minutes, and I see you looking away when I'm trying to present my arguments [Observation]. I am feeling frustrated and disappointed [Feeling]. I need to know that we understand each other and I need your support on this project [Need]. I would like you to listen to my proposal and my reasoning [Request]. If you do that then I will be more than happy to do my best to understand your thinking on this issue [Exchange]."

Compare this with:

"John, can't you ever stop talking and listen for just this once?"

Your "Comfort Zone" and Your Style of Influencing

We have been brought up by parents and other care-givers to become proper adults, who will fit easily into the culture in which we live. In order to be loved, liked, accepted and respected by those around us, we learn what is acceptable and what is not. Our behaviour is in part the product of accumulated learning from the past. We have received countless messages from our parents, our friends, our social, ethnic, cultural, religious and family environments which stimulate and support some behaviours, while discouraging and inhibiting others. Behaviours which were considered acceptable were internalised, and define the range of behaviours we call the *comfort zone*. Behaviours which were considered unacceptable came to fall outside our comfort zone.

However great the value and importance of everything we learned as we grew up, those same lessons can also inhibit or reduce our effectiveness in the organisational environment in which we find ourselves today. What we learned, usually without question, can inhibit and restrain us, and prevent us from achieving the kind of behavioural flexibility we seek – and require – in order to be effective in the situations we face today.

Here is an example of a series of messages, which might continue to resonate, largely subconsciously, in the mind of a young man growing up in a Western culture. These messages helped him to learn what was okay and not okay in the eyes of others, and they now define, in part, his comfort zone.

- Look after "number one";
- Nice guys finish last;
- Winning isn't the most important thing; it's the *only* thing;
- Real men don't eat quiche (drink vermouth, go to the ballet etc...);
- Crying is a sign of weakness;
- Do unto others before they do unto you;
- People don't have to like you as long as they respect you;
- Take a stand and make your mark.

These messages continue to resonate in his subconscious or semiconscious, and determine the comfort zone. As a result, it is likely that he:

- doesn't show his emotions easily;
- has trouble really listening to others' views and aspirations;

- sets very high personal goals and targets for himself – and feels inadequate if he doesn't achieve them;
- tends to bully people who disagree with him;
- always wants to have the last word;
- has difficulty making real connections with people and hence feels alone and sometimes misunderstood.

Placed in situations in which it is perfectly reasonable to expect him to understand the aspirations of others, generate team spirit, let others take the credit, share feelings (especially negative ones like sadness or inadequacy), set realistic personal goals, or ask for help, those messages from his past act like elastic bands. They pull him back into his comfort zone and limit the potential for effective action.

The following questions may help you to become aware of your own comfort zone and to look at the changes that might be necessary to improve your ability to influence others and your chances of success in a new, future role.

- How would your comfort zone look if you mapped it out on a three-dimensional model?

THE COMFORT ZONE

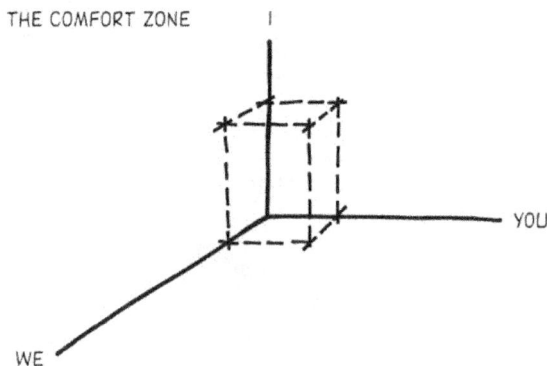

YOU

WE

- Are you comfortable in the *I-dimension* but do you sometimes hear that you should let others speak more often?
- Are you fine with listening carefully to others, but get the advice that you should take charge of discussions more often?
- In what ways would you like to change/expand your comfort zone?
- What behaviours do not require your attention, because you are already skilful enough in using them?
- Which behaviours should you pay more attention to?
- What would you like to try out in order to see if you can make it work and whether it "fits" you in your current role?

The influence model is not meant to suggest that there is such a thing as "ideal behaviour". To what extent the behaviours of each dimension are indeed necessary will depend on the environment in which you work or relate to others. The comfort zone you might map out while thinking of home would very probably look quite different from what you would map out while thinking of work, but all three dimensions are important. You need to be able to move into each one. Once upon a time you did have all that flexibility but in the course of your life you have closed some doors...

The Castle[18]

Imagine being a magnificent castle with long hallways and thousands of rooms. Every room in the castle is perfect and possesses a special gift. Each room represents a different aspect of yourself and is an integral part of the entire perfect castle. As a child, you explored every inch of your castle without shame or judgment. Fearlessly you searched every room for its jewels and its mystery. Lovingly you embraced every room whether it was a closet, a bedroom, bathroom, or a cellar. Each and every room was unique. Your castle was full of light, love, and wonder. Then one day, someone came to your castle and told you that one of your rooms was imperfect, that surely it didn't belong in your castle. They suggested that if you wanted to have a perfect castle you should close and lock the door to this room. Since you wanted love and acceptance, you quickly closed off that room. From that time on, you closed more and more doors for all kinds of reasons. You closed doors because you were afraid, or you thought the rooms were too bold. You closed doors to rooms that were too conservative. You closed doors because other castles you saw did not have a room like yours. It just became a habit. Shutting off those rooms actually started to make you feel safe. You soon found yourself living in just a few small rooms. You had learned how to shut off life and became comfortable doing it. Many of us also locked away so many rooms that we forgot we were ever a castle. We began to believe that we were just a small, two-bedroom house in need of repairs.

---

[18]From Debbie Ford, *The Dark Side of the Light Chasers*, 1999.

It is important to rediscover what was once available to you, what you have forgotten and is necessary for you in this phase of your life. This will ensure that your way of speaking and influencing will remain yours. You do not need to renounce your true self. On the contrary, you will finally become who you really are. This is not to say that you will always behave the same way. That is because each friend or colleague or situation requires something else of you. Being yourself means you can behave differently in different situations. Sometimes you will have to make yourself heard strongly, at other moments you will need to show your own vulnerability.

Experimentation and Reflection

Behaviour Questionnaire

In Appendix 1 you will find a short questionnaire which you can use to map out your own use of the different behaviours. In order to get as balanced a picture as possible it can be useful to invite people who know you in different settings (at work, at home, colleagues, manager, client) to complete it as well. You might even look for people with whom you have different kinds of relationships (smooth, difficult). Of course, complete one for yourself too, maybe more than one, reflecting how you think you behave in different situations.

Examine the total result. Is the distribution across the different groups of questions recognisable? Do others' scores generally coincide with your own? If not, what conclusions can you draw?

If you look at the results from different people, where are the differences? Can you relate differences to corresponding differences in the relationship? Are the results very similar across the board? That could indicate a lack of flexibility.

The results only give an indication, but they can help you to think about, and work on, your behavioural repertoire. Remember also that people differ with regard to the ease with which they give high or low scores. Some people go for extremes, while others are more reserved or cautious. Often they take their own comfort with a behaviour as a reference point. In the eyes of someone who moves easily in the *I-dimension* you might not come across as very strong, whereas someone else may feel that you take and defend positions emphatically. As people also reveal a lot about themselves while answering the questionnaire, it is wise to thank them for their trouble. A conversation with a respondent after he or she has completed the questionnaire can also help you to interpret results. Nothing is quite as useful as a discussion with someone who experiences you frequently, about your behaviour and its impact.

Make notes for yourself about the most important messages you have received, and the insights you gained.

Don't Lead Yourself Down the Garden Path!

The pictures you have of yourself and of your influence behaviour and effectiveness are strongly distorted by psychological tendencies that are deeply ingrained in the human mind. It is hardly surprising that others see you in a different way from how you see yourself. It is important to understand the tendencies which might play a role for you. Consider them as an invitation to make use of others' perceptions of you in your search for more effective behaviour.

1. The tendency to rate yourself as better than average is known as the **Lake Wobegon effect**. This effect is named after a fictional town of Garrison Keillor's radio reports,

News from Lake Wobegon, where "all women are strong, all men are handsome and all children above average".

2. The **egocentric bias** makes us see ourselves as the centre of the world, and leads us to underestimate the contributions and capacities of others. For example, if you ask a couple about their share of household work, together they will invariably come up with more than 100%: both partners see themselves as doing more than the other.

3. The **spotlight effect** leads us to believe that others pay as much attention to our appearance and behaviour as we do. Does everyone notice that you are wearing a new sweater, or have a pimple on your chin? Forget it – everyone (just like you) is too busy focusing on himself.

4. The **false consensus effect** leads us to believe that others are more like us than they really are. Heavy drinkers tend to overestimate the number of people who drink as much as they do.

5. The **confirmation bias** is the tendency to search for information that will confirm an existing idea or image. This leads us to overlook information that proves the opposite, as a result of which we will not easily change our views, including those, which we hold about ourselves.

6. The **hindsight bias**, also known as the "I thought so" effect, allows us to continue to overestimate ourselves. If you lose your money to a back-alley mugger you will not readily admit that you should have been more careful. It is easier to believe that you "had the feeling" right away that it was a dodgy neighbourhood.

7. The **fundamental attribution error** is the general tendency of people to overestimate the influence of a

single person on an event, and to underestimate the role of the circumstances. If we see someone stumble and fall, we tend first to think that the person was clumsy, not that the pavement might have been slippery.

8. The **actor-observer bias** leads us to ascribe to their personality, the events that overcome others ("he got beaten up because he is always looking for trouble"). What happens to us is blamed on the situation. Individuals know that they respond differently in different situations; they do not know this about others.

9. The **self-serving bias** allows us to ascribe positive outcomes to our own abilities, and negative outcomes to the situation. This helps to maintain a positive self-image.

10. He who believes that he is less a victim of these blind spots than others, is the victim of the **ultimate self-serving bias**. A funny paradox, really: research shows that most people believe themselves to be less susceptible to psychological distortions than others.

The human mind is an over-confidence machine. The conscious level gives itself credit for things it didn't really do and fabricates imaginary experiences to create the illusion it controls things it doesn't determine. 90% of drivers believe they are above average behind the wheel. 94% of college professors think they are above-average teachers. 90% of entrepreneurs think their new business will be a success. 98% of students [in the USA] who take the SAT tests say they have average or above average leadership skills.[19]

---

[19]David Brooks, *The Social Animal*, 2011. 218

Recognising Dimensions and Behaviours

Imagine that someone makes the following statements to you. For each statement, write down which Dimension of influence behaviour the person is using and then, within the Dimension, which specific behaviour is being used.

Bear in mind that the impact of a verbal statement is also determined by the non-verbal behaviour which accompanies it (tone of voice, expression, gestures). Your answers will sometimes reflect the tone of voice, expression and gestures which you imagine the speaker using, and there may be more than one correct answer.

1. That was an excellent presentation you made this afternoon!

2. How much time will you need in order to complete the report?

3. I don't know how best to handle this situation; it would really help me if someone could help to sort this out.

4. There are two reasons why I cannot agree with your proposal. The first is... and the second is...

5. How do you feel about the changes that were suggested this morning?

6. That's probably the silliest idea I have ever heard!

7. Let me see if I understand your thinking on this: in your view the key issue is the problem we're having with the z-module, and what we need to do is focus all our attention there first. Have I understood you correctly?

8. Okay, I will commit to getting the text of the report done by Thursday afternoon. But the graphics will have to wait until next week.

9. Your reaction is a bit over the top, but I can imagine that you feel yourself seriously disadvantaged.
10. Why don't we try to sort this out with Purchasing?

For possible answers see page 86

Responding Flexibly to Others

In principle we always have a choice regarding how we respond to someone else: which Dimension and which specific Behaviour to use. This does not imply that each behaviour will be equally appropriate at every moment during a discussion. But we do have a choice, and in order to make the best choice and respond in the most appropriate manner we need to develop flexibility.

Imagine someone saying each of the following things to you. Then write down how you could respond using each of the behaviours indicated.

For example:

I think you're missing the point entirely here. You don't seem to have understood the seriousness of the problem.

a *You-dimension*, Asking response: "Help me to understand how you view the problem."
b *We-dimension*, Disclosing Needs response: "Okay; I need some help here!"
c *I-dimension*, Declaring response: "I value your frankness, and I don't appreciate your tone of voice."

1. I'm feeling depressed by the way things have been going recently. We're just not moving forward; we're obviously stuck somewhere.

a   *You-dimension*, Listening response

b   *I-dimension*, Requesting response

c   *We-dimension*, Acknowledging response

2. I'm really extremely rushed at the moment; I'm under a lot of pressure. I don't see how I can help you with that report. Sorry!

   a.   *We-dimension*, Acknowledging

   b.   *I-dimension*, Requesting

   c.   *I-dimension*, Reasoning

3. You are absolutely wrong in your assessment of the situation! You really need to think things through more carefully before making a proposal.

   a.   *You-dimension*, Asking

   b.   *I-dimension*, Requesting

   c.   *We-dimension*, Disclosing Needs

4. I'd like you to make time in your agenda to handle the XYZ-account from now on. This has a high priority for our department.

   a.   *I-dimension*, Promising

   b.   *You-dimension*, Listening

   c.   *We-dimension*, Sharing Feelings

5. We need to reorganise our priorities. I think we should put less energy into unpredictable client X and focus ourselves on creating a better long-term market strategy.

   a.   *I-dimension*, Reasoning

   b.   *I-dimension*, Declaring

   c.   *We-dimension*, Acknowledging

For possible answers see page 86

Experimenting with the I-dimension

The following suggestions can help you to sharpen up or extend your *I-dimension* behaviours.

- *Requesting*: Think of something that someone could do for you that would make your work easier or make the relationship more satisfying for you. Create an opportunity to ask that this person to do this – and then do so. Avoid justifying your request with reasons; let the Request do its work.

- *Reasoning*: Think of a current social or political issue about which you have strong views. Write down *concisely* what your views are, and why. Now create an appropriate opportunity to express your views powerfully and clearly to a friend or colleague.

- *Promising*: Think of something, which you know that a friend or colleague would like you to start doing, do more, or do differently. Think carefully about what you *are* and/or *are not* prepared to do. Find an opportunity to state clearly what the friend or colleague can expect of you in terms of compliance and/or non-compliance with his or her wishes.

- *Declaring*: Think of something, which someone did or said recently which you really appreciated or valued. Did you express your appreciation fully? What could you have said to make your feelings clear and explicit? Now call or go to the person involved and say what you have to say. Turning it around, did that someone say or do something to upset you? How could you have told the other person, without a lot of explanation, that what he said or did was unacceptable?

- *Declaring*: What is your vision regarding what your part of the organisation could be like in five years? Find the words to express this in some detail, and present your vision with enthusiasm at an appropriate moment. Make it clear that you believe in what you are saying. Make clear that you expect your listener(s) to work with you towards achieving the goal. Don't explain or reason; see what the effect of your words is.

Experimenting with the You-dimension

- Think of someone in your immediate environment with whom you disagree strongly regarding a current social or political issue. Use your next meeting with this person exclusively to ask about and understand his or her views.
- Try to discover what especially motivates or "drives" someone at work. Don't be satisfied with a quick answer; ask follow-up questions to probe more deeply.
- Think of someone who has a clear preference for a certain type of music, preferably different from your own. The next time you have the opportunity to do so, try to discover what this music does for or means to the other person.
- Think of someone with whom you have regular disagreements or conflicts. Write down as many things as you can think of, which you don't understand about the person (beliefs, behaviours, values...). Think of what questions you could ask this person, which, if answered, would help you to understand the person better.
- The next time someone mentions with enthusiasm a movie or play which he has seen or a book which she or he has read, try to find out just *what* it was about the movie, play or book which generated such enthusiasm.

- Identify someone with whom you have worked closely for some time. Try to find out how this person *really* thinks and feels about you as a colleague.

Experimenting with the We-dimension

If you are sensitive to the opportunities which life offers, it will not be difficult to find occasions when it would benefit your relationship with another person to increase the level of mutual trust. This requires being open to the other person about your feelings and needs, *and* being open to the feelings and needs of the other person. Here are several suggestions which might help you to practice the relevant behaviours.

- The next time you feel the need to receive some help with something, whether personal or work-related, *tell* an appropriate person that you need help, rather than simply thinking about it and carrying on in an attempt to make the best of it without assistance.
- Take a blank sheet of paper and write down all the words denoting feelings which you are aware of having experienced over the last twenty-four hours. Make a distinction between positive and negative feelings. In the case of negative feelings, which needs were not being met? What sort of help do you need in order that the frustrated needs be better met? In the case of positive feelings, which needs were being met? With whom would you be willing to share your analyses? Do so!
- When someone expresses a viewpoint with which you tend to disagree, find a way of expressing your acceptance of this point of view as being legitimate and understandable given the other person's experiences, needs or interests.

- Think of a colleague with whom you have a number of things in common, like ambitions, interests, dreams, concerns, hopes and fears. Use a next opportunity to *tell* the other person what you feel you have in common.
- Virtually everyone experiences self-doubt from time to time, usually related to specific situations. Rather than keeping these doubts to yourself, try sharing your thoughts and feelings at an appropriate moment with a friend or colleague with whom you feel sufficient trust to try this.

Switching Between Dimensions: Managing Irritation

Earlier (pages 64-68) you read about a five-step method of managing irritation. The following questions will help you to respond to a situation in which you were previously irritated, in a calm, controlled manner, by moving between the *I-dimension* and the *We-dimension*.

- Call to mind a situation in which someone irritated you with his or her behaviour. Try to remember what you were doing during this event. Write this down. Now remember exactly what you observed, with your eyes and ears. What was it exactly, which triggered your irritation? What could you say to the other about what you observed – in neutral words, without judging or accusing. Write this down in the form: "X, I saw/heard that you…"
- Identify the feeling(s) which you experienced when observing this behaviour. Add this to the sentence which you have just written down: "I saw/heard that you… I then felt…" (See also a list of words naming feelings in Appendix 2.)

- Realise that negative feelings arise when needs are frustrated. Which need lay behind your feelings? What could you have said about this to the other. Continue what you have written down with: "I need/would like..." (See the list of possible needs in Appendix 2.)
- What request could you express to the other person which, if accepted, would help to ensure that your need is met? Continue what you have written down with: "I would ask you in the future to..." Look for your own words. Make sure that your feelings and needs come across, without drifting into a judgment or accusation.
- Think of what need(s) of the other might lie behind what you see or hear him or her do or say. What could you offer the other person in exchange. How can you put this into words, in a clear and personal manner.
- Now speak the whole chain of four or five sentences out loud. How do you experience this way of speaking?

Exploring and Expanding your Comfort Zone

Your current behavioural flexibility is limited by the messages you have picked up in the past. They stimulate some behaviours and repress others, and as result that zone of influence behaviour develops, within which you feel comfortable. The question is whether these behaviours will still be sufficient in the next step in your career. That's why it is worth the effort to map out your own comfort zone and identify the key messages that gave shape to it. In this way you become aware of the implicit choices you make and as a result you acquire the opportunity to make the changes you want.

Make a list of all the implicit and explicit "messages" from the past that come to mind. These consist of remarks or experiences that linger in your memory, and can be as vague as a recollection of the way someone looked at you after you did or said something. They might come from parents, other family members, street pals, teachers, colleagues, managers or other role models. You recognise them as having been formative influences for your comfort zone. Do this in peace and quiet; take whatever time is necessary.

Which messages were really important for determining your comfort zone? What benefit have you gained from? Which could be important if you think about your next career step? Which would you like to leave behind now? What or who could help you in this? If possible, share your analysis with someone whom you trust and who is also willing to make this sort of analysis. The following four steps, derived from the *We-dimension*, can help you to ensure that a discussion is mutually beneficial.

1. *Sharing feelings*: Tell each other which messages from the past are now determining the boundaries of your comfort zone. Tell each other if and when you have experienced the restrictive effect of these (old) messages during a recent conversation with which you felt less than satisfied. How did you feel at such a moment?

2. *Disclosing needs*: What do you need which would help you to discard now irrelevant messages from the past? What suggestions and experiences does your partner have?

3. *Acknowledging*: Tell in which way you recognise yourself in each other's stories.

4. *Reflection*: What was it like to engage in this discussion? Do you see any things which could be relevant in your work?

Possible answers to questions on p.77-78:

1. *I-dimension* – Declaring
2. *I-dimension* – Requesting (information)
3. *We-dimension* – Disclosing Needs
4. *I-dimension* – Reasoning
5. *You-dimension* – Asking
6. Negative Behaviour – putting someone down
7. *You-dimension* – Listening
8. *I-dimension* – Promising
9. *We-dimension* – Acknowledging
10. *I-dimension* – Requesting

Possible answers to questions on p.78-79:

1a: "You sound very worried. I am right in understanding that you would like someone to make a decision?"

1b: "Okay, I suggest you stop your work on this project and help John with his tests."

1c: "I'm concerned too, and I can certainly understand that you are upset by not seeing a way forward."

2a: "I can see that you're overwhelmed at the moment; I wouldn't be able to focus on something else either. I'll see if Frank can help."

2b: "I want you to have another look at your – and our – priorities. You really need to look at this."

2c: "There are two reasons why I need you to look at this report. First..., second... Besides, the XYZ project you're into can really wait a week or so. It's not that urgent."

3a: "Please help me to understand what you think I've missed, and where your strong concern is coming from."

3b: "I'd like you to tell me what criteria you are using to make your judgment."

3c: "I need help to understand the wider implications here."

4a: "Okay, I'll pick it up next week, when I have finished my contribution to our new website."

4b: "Do I understand that you think I should put the website development on hold for a while, that it has a lower priority?"

4c: "Terrific! That is a great opportunity and I'm really excited about it. I am worried about whether or not I have sufficient experience, though."

5a: "Given the current uncertainty in the market I doubt whether it would be wise to focus on the long-term right now. In addition, if we meet X's expectations fully in the short-term then it will significantly increase our chances with other clients in the medium term."

5b: "I think that's a foolish suggestion. Our first priority is *always* to put customer satisfaction first."

5c: "I understand that you might wish to shift priorities. Given your responsibilities, I understand the importance of the long term."

3

THE NATURE OF TRUST

"Trust me! I know I'm right about this!"
"Of course; I trust all my people."
"We have to trust each other!"
"Trust yourself."

The word *trust* is used easily, frequently – and sometimes carelessly – as the brief sentences above demonstrate. How frequently do we stop to think about what the word really means? Do we accord the concept sufficient justice? Trust is absolutely central to the creation and maintenance of positive working relationships. Creating trust is essential if you wish to influence others effectively. For this reason we devote a separate chapter to it in this book.

Building trust is a skill, which can be learned. "To trust is to take on the personal responsibility of making a commitment."[20] Trust

---

[20]*Robert C. Solomon & Fernando Flores. Building trust in business, politics, relationships and life,* Oxford University Press, 2001. (Page 45)

is generated when the other experiences us being clear and speaking with integrity (*I-dimension*), when the other experiences us as showing true interest (*You-dimension*) and when the other experiences us as respectful with regard to his or her feelings and needs and sees us as open about our own (*We-dimension*).

As soon as we start to look at *trust* more carefully, we find that it is almost impossible to define satisfactorily. Ask someone what *trust* is and there is a likelihood that the answer will incorporate platitudes and clichés. If building or creating trust is important then it is necessary to understand what it means. We begin by demonstrating the crucial difference between being *trustworthy* and *reliable*.

Trust and Reliability

A while ago the CIO of a telecom company (Ph.D. in Physics and Mathematics) came to one of us to reflect on his leadership style. In his early forties, he had enjoyed an enviable career – so far. In a recent appraisal he was, however, rated as less than excellent. This disappointing appraisal preoccupied him. He couldn't really understand it. On the one hand his subordinates respected and admired him greatly. He was very decisive, bright, quick and clear. On the other hand his subordinates kept their distance from him, and seemed to be slightly suspicious of him. They seemed to wonder, "What does he really want?" "What does he think of us?" While his managers, the Board members, regarded him very highly as a trouble-shooter and fixer, they considered him to be insensitive to the diplomatic niceties required to get things done with other stakeholders. "They don't really trust me!" he concluded. When asked: "How do you work on this?" he replied: "I always keep my promises and stick to my commitments." That was his idea about building trust.

The CIO was confusing two things: *trust* and *reliability*. He is not the only one to do so. These concepts appear very similar and they are frequently used interchangeably. The difference is fortunately easy to clarify. Consider the following two pairs of statements:

You are reliable – I trust you.

This is my most reliable subordinate – I trust this subordinate completely.

What, precisely, is the difference? The word *trust* has been defined as follows:

a: assured reliance on the character, ability, strength, or truth of someone or something

b: one in whom confidence is placed[21]

When we say that we trust someone, we have confidence in his character, and often we also assume that we share the same or similar outlook and values. We will trust such a person even if he is not always as punctual or accurate as others. Reliability and predictability are important components of trust, but not decisive. Simply living up to agreements is not the key issue. In order to gain trust we need to talk about and share our ideas, viewpoints, and opinions about things. Trust includes reliability but involves much more.[22] It includes *like-mindedness* as well as reliability.

---

[21] trust. (2008). In *Merriam-Webster Online Dictionary*. Retrieved October 1, 2008, from http://www.merriam-webster.com/dictionary/trust

[22] See also: Patrick Lencioni, *The Five Dysfunctions of a Team*. Jossey-Bass, 2002

The Loss of Trust

We will look at how trust works in personal relationships. Sometimes trust is only recognised when it has been damaged or lost.

Different Viewpoints

Edward and Balaji, colleague middle-managers in a multinational organisation, got on well from the time they first met. Differences in national and cultural background did not seem to interfere with what quickly grew into a warm friendship. They visited each other's homes and families.

When their company entered a difficult period due to an economic recession, all managers felt the pressure. Balaji put extra effort into his group of direct reports, believing strongly in the importance of "human capital" and believing that his team could come up with the necessary results as long as they were inspired and motivated. Edward saw his first priority as cutting costs.

When he told Balaji that he was releasing one-third of his group, Balaji couldn't believe his ears and reacted rather explosively. Balaji asked himself how he could trust someone who could act so ruthlessly towards his own people, and expressed his dismay openly to Edward. Edward felt that he was doing the right thing and felt rather proud of himself for being able to make tough decisions. He asked himself whether he could really trust Balaji enough to discuss his actions with him openly. Their friendship cooled considerably as they started to see each other in a very different light.

Trust is, among other things, about believing that you and another person share basic values. We easily assume that someone with whom we intuitively feel a strong connection shares our basic values. However, until they are tested there is no way to know for sure. While it is not an issue, it isn't generally talked about. This results in a sort of illusory trust. But talking about values, sharing one's own and listening to and respecting another person's, are fundamental steps towards building and maintaining trust. This sharing does of course carry the risk that some fundamental differences may be uncovered.

Balaji reacted very strongly. Why? When someone whom you trust seems to behave in a manner, which contradicts your cherished principles, this can cause your trust, also in yourself, to become shaky. You may start to ask yourself whether the values that are dear to you are indeed valid. Within intensive relationships this can cause deep distress, as is illustrated in the following example.

An evening amongst friends

Juliette, an outgoing, extravert sort, and Nicole, a rather shy and quiet person, gradually became close friends after Nicole joined the company. Juliette took it upon herself to make Nicole feel comfortable by joining her for lunch on several occasions and even inviting her out for a drink after work on a Friday evening. Nicole felt very fortunate and happy with Juliette's attention. In spite of their different characters, they discovered that they had many interests in common, and the friendship grew.

After a number of months Juliette decided to invite Nicole to an evening social gathering of a number of close friends. She felt that it would be good for Nicole, who had moved from another city just before joining the company, to meet more people. Nicole accepted gratefully.

When the anticipated evening came, Nicole in fact felt rather uncomfortable. She found it difficult to initiate conversation with strangers and felt herself to be an outsider. Her discomfort grew as the evening passed. Juliette and the others all seemed to be having a wonderful time, with lots of laughter. Juliette and Nicole made occasional eye contact with Juliette smiling encouragingly, while Nicole had difficulty forcing a smile onto her face. She felt herself to be abandoned. She also realised that she had counted too much on Juliette's attention and that Juliette was not able to offer it because she had so many other friends there. Nicole became increasingly uncomfortable. She felt herself to be a bother and in the way, particularly for Juliette. Half way through the evening she quietly fetched her coat and, mumbling a feeble excuse, said goodbye and slipped out the front door. Juliette was surprised but of course let her go.

When they saw each other at work the next

Monday, Juliette was furious with Nicole, and said she felt betrayed by her. Nicole was totally taken aback by Juliette's anger, thinking that she had acted in Juliette's best interests, and retreated into her shell. That in turn confirmed Juliette's perception that Nicole was ungrateful, because she wanted to know what had really happened for Nicole, but wasn't getting any answers.

Juliette and Nicole remained upset for some time, and the friendship never fully recovered.

By not trusting in the loyalty and warmth of Juliette, Nicole lost a large measure of the trust that she so much craved. She didn't trust others because she didn't trust herself enough to ask for help. She had grown up with a feeling of not being very likeable or worthwhile or as having much to offer, and that old pattern of thinking and feeling had welled up again during the party.

What made it impossible for Nicole to discuss openly with Juliette her feelings of possibly being a burden? Why did she choose *not* to talk? (In Chapter 1 we discussed the necessity of talking.) Why couldn't Nicole do it here? Perhaps there was a desire for autonomy: this time I will make a decision for myself! The threat to trust here, lies in attempting to think for the other person: thinking what the other person probably wants, that the other person will understand, that the other person even expects you to make your own decision. At the same time, this "thinking for the other person" results in not truly thinking for yourself; you fail to sort out exactly what it is that is causing your own irritation – or other negative feeling.

Probably Nicole was not able to accept her own irritation:

Juliette should after all have known it would be difficult for her. She mistrusted her own motives: was she leaving to meet her own needs or for Juliette's sake? Self-awareness requires acknowledging that we are not perfect, that we are sometimes aggressive in our behaviours, and sometimes childish. Not being blind to your shadow-side is important for not being blind to the shadow-sides of others. Accepting yourself – with your own imperfections – makes it possible to accept others with their imperfections. This two-way acceptance makes dialogue possible.

It is not possible to believe in others when one doesn't believe in oneself. It is not possible to trust in others if one doesn't trust oneself. Nicole did not have faith in herself, and therefore quickly saw herself as being a burden, and lost trust in Juliette's sincere effort to make her feel welcome and included.

Nicole didn't discuss her misguided decision to slip quietly away, she took it based on her assumptions about how others thought and felt. At the same time, Juliette made assumptions or personal interpretations about what was driving Nicole in her actions and reacted correspondingly. Trust cannot be built or maintained on the basis of assumptions. Fundamental to building and maintaining trust is the willingness and ability to share one's own thoughts and feelings, and to enquire after and listen to the thoughts and feelings of others. Trust is built and based on openness – openness about oneself, and openness towards the other. Closing oneself off and basing actions on assumptions about what someone else may think or feel destroys trust, damages relationships and hurts individuals, sometimes deeply.

Edward and Balaji, Juliette and Nicole – they lost trust in each other, which was painful because they had felt that they could trust each other implicitly. However, trust cannot ever be considered a given; it must be renewed and strengthened constantly. To ignore breakdowns or to eventually forget about them is always dangerous. Occurrences like those described above are never completely forgotten; if they are not thoroughly and openly talked through they will remain threats to the future of any relationship, whether in a work context, a social context or – perhaps most of all – in a very personal context.

Rebuilding trust after a breakdown requires a great deal of effort, a great deal of disclosing and enquiring. Such an effort is not possible when both parties succumb to their own negative feelings and, in Nicole's case, lose all trust in themselves.

Rebuilding Trust

Trust is not a "thing", something which you can lose, which is either there or it is not. That is an oversimplification. If people talk about the fragility of trust they do the phenomenon no justice. Trust is then likened to a vase which, once broken, can never be returned to its original state. When trust is lost it is not irreparable. It can be restored, and can actually be deepened by the crisis it went through.

Trust is an outcome of social interaction. It is co-created. It can be seen as a decision (or as a series of decisions) which opens the world to us and deepens relationships. It creates new possibilities, even new worlds. Trust is something that we can and must work on. Establishing one's reliability helps us to become seen as trustworthy (again). In addition to this we need to be able to talk about trust or its absence in an open, non-defensive manner. Trust is a result of making connection.

Executive Coach Judith E. Glaser wrote:

The ability to work together inter-dependently is one of our least-developed skills. This is so vital that, in its absence, good leaders turn bad, good executives become ineffective, and good colleagues turn into adversaries. The skill of opening up to others – and of creating the emotional space for others to open up to – requires deep trust. ... When we experience doubt about the good intentions of others, for whatever reason, we need to recognise the importance of having the kind of conversations that bring us back to trust. Creating the space for open dialogues enables us to reclaim trust with others.[23]

Open dialogue between adults can result in the rebuilding of trust. That is Judith Glaser's message. We need to learn to live with the inevitability of inter-dependence. That will only succeed if authentic trust exists between us. In order to achieve this we will need to learn to be open to strangers, people we do not – or hardly – know.

What can we do?

When you give people the following incomplete sentence and ask which verb is missing: *Trust is something you must...* in five out of six cases people will choose "earn". (The reader may wish to test out this hypothesis in his or her own environment!) This confirms the argument above that many people consider trust to be the equivalent of reliability. Steven Covey seemed to write about trust in this sense when he described the process of building an "Emotional Bank Account" through courtesy, kindness, honesty *and keeping commitments*[24] (our italics). But

---

[23] Judith E. Glaser: *Creating WE*, 2005. 176

[24] Steven R. Covey: *The 7 Habits of Highly Effective People*. 1990. 188

he also implied an alternative point of view: that trust is not simply about earning but also about giving (in his words), kindness and honesty. Put another way, one might say that trust is co-created rather than earned or given.

Consider the example of a manager who, for the first time, gives a young employee the responsibility for carrying out a major task. He offers this person his trust. This changes the employee: he takes a next step towards the development of a sense of responsibility for his or her work. And it changes the manager: he comes closer to assuming a place as his employee's equal. Giving trust changes both parties to the exchange. Their relationship deepens: a sense of partnership starts to develop. In that relationship trust goes much deeper than reliability. The manager does not yet know if he can rely on his employee, but he gives him trust. The manager does not offer trust blindly. He has come to know his employee to some extent, and he knows himself. He knows to choose the right moment at which to give responsibility and the trust. The wise manager also learns to give trust in stages, risking a little at a time, so that if trust is broken, the damage can be mended. This is a form of trust which we can call "authentic trust".

There is a striking parallel between the concepts of *trust* and *love*; love, also, is something which we *give*, rather than *earn*. Roger Harrison was probably the first prominent consultant to dare to use the word *love* in the workplace, preferring it to euphemisms such as *caring* or *consideration*. He might have described the example of the manager and the young employee as one in which the manager empowered his junior through letting him or her experience a strong feeling of positive value:[25]

When we experience love, we tend to become both responsive
and responsible. We care, we take care of things, organizations,
and people we love.

Authentic trust and love are closely related concepts; reliability
and love are not.

Forms of Trust

It is useful to distinguish between different forms of trust. The
word *trust* carries many meanings and the question is, what
exactly do you need to aim for if you wish to build trust in a
business environment. Not every form of trust is desirable. Robert
Solomon and Fernando Flores, a distinguished philosopher and a
well-known businessman and politician distinguished between
simple trust, blind trust and *authentic trust.*[26]

Simple trust

This is a form of trust, which is unthinking and unreflective,
which we are all born with. Simple trust, sometimes called *thin
trust*, is marked by an utter absence of suspicion. On the one
hand, it makes it possible to function in day-to-day life. We
have to trust people we don't even know, whether we like it or
not. When driving, we trust the other drivers on the road to
act according to the rules. When asking directions in an

---

[25]Roger Harrison, "Empowerment in Organizations" (1985), in *Collected
Papers*, 1995 and "Accessing the Power of Love in the Workplace",
unpublished paper, 2008

[26]*Robert C. Solomon & Fernando Flores. Building trust in business, politics,
relationships and life,* 2001

unfamiliar town, we trust a person to give us correct directions. In a world of virtual teams and tele-conferences with individuals we have probably never met we have to trust that what is said is true and that commitments made will be kept. But in more complex interaction, it is not enough. Simple trust is not true trust any more than first (and equally naïve) love is true love.[27] At some point simple or naïve trust is shattered, and can give way to a pervasive distrust. It does not seem coincidental that virtual teams are generally ineffective unless members have the opportunity to meet each other face-to-face at least twice a year. A former Senior Vice-President of Digital Equipment Corporation, David L. Stone, said in the 1980s that "the half life of trust is three months", meaning that individuals were required to undertake transatlantic travel to meet their colleagues and counterparts that frequently.[28]

Blind trust

This form of trust equates trust with absolute trust. Blind trust is uncritical and unquestioning. It is like blind faith: it cannot be diminished by evidence which would show that it is unfounded. We close our eyes and refuse to see such facts. Blind trust is sometimes demanded (but not given!) by corporate and political, as well as religious, leaders. Giving in to the demand and ignoring the evidence makes it a form of self-deception. Blind trust is powerful and seductive: it appears to offer certainty in an extremely complex world, it releases us from doubt and it offers us heroes and heavens.

---

[27]*Ibid*. Page 62

[28]Reported by our colleague, Jeremy Scanlan

Authentic trust

"Trust in the face of doubts and concerns, trust in the world of uncertainty, is authentic trust."[29] In the course of our lives we learn that simple trust can be betrayed. That does not mean that you need to become cynical and disavow the trusting of others forever. You will have to continue trusting, but not naively. You are aware of the risks and dangers involved in giving trust. Nevertheless, you choose to trust. Authentic trust, also called *thick trust*, is a committed openness; "to trust someone is not to say 'anything goes' but rather to keep open one's responses, [and] expectations."[30] Authentic trust, that openness to another person, is a function of human interaction and has to be *given*.

Trust and Society

Two particular items struck the authors while writing an early draft of this chapter. One was background coverage relating to the fall of a major financial institution, even before the worldwide financial crisis of 2008 had fully developed. The analysts found at least part of the cause for the debacle in a deep mistrust of one another which reportedly reigned among the senior officers of the organisation shortly before it fell. The second item came in a history book, about the chaos during and shortly after the Chinese Cultural Revolution in the 1960s. The chaos was driven in great part by a deep sense of mistrust between the leaders of the Chinese Communist Party (CCP) and the leaders of the People's Liberation Army (PLA).[31]

---

[29]*Ibid*. Page 62

[30]*Ibid*. Page 55

[31]Jonathan D. Spence: *The Search for Modern China*. 1991.

Organisations, large and small, cannot survive in good health when its members do not trust each other authentically. Neither can a society. Building trust is an on-going challenge, with measurable pay-offs: "Students of public health find that life expectancy itself is enhanced in more trustful communities." [32]

Extensive research has suggested that a nation's prosperity and its ability to compete are dependent on a key cultural attribute: the level of trust shown towards strangers, individuals from outside the family or clan.[33] "Trusting communities, other things being equal, have a measurable economic advantage."[34]

Virtually all economic activity in the contemporary world is carried out not by individuals but by organizations that require a high degree of social cooperation. Property rights, contracts, and commercial law are all indispensable institutions for creating a modern market-oriented economic system, but it is possible to economize substantially on transaction costs if such institutions are supplemented by social capital and trust.[35]

---

[32]Robert D. Putnam, *Bowling Alone*. 2000. Page135

[33]An ironic footnote: while preparing this draft the authors, like so many others, were spending a great deal of time following the news of the world financial crisis of September/October 2008 and the following recession. Repeatedly, news analysts pointed out that citizens had lost their trust in the financial institutions, while those same institutions had lost trust in each other. The world teetered on the brink of economic collapse.

[34]Robert D. Putnam, op.cit. Page135

[35]Francis Fukayama, *Trust, The Social Virtues and the Creation of Prosperity*. 1995. Pages 335-336

These words are echoed by another, more recent writer:

Trust is habitual reciprocity that becomes coated by emotion. It grows when two people begin volleys of communication and cooperation and slowly learn they can rely upon each other. Soon members of a trusting relationship become willing to not only cooperate with each other but sacrifice for each other.

Trust reduces friction and lowers transaction costs. People in companies filled with trust move flexibly and cohesively. People who live in trusting cultures form more community organizations. People in more trusting organizations have wider stock-market participation rates. People in trusting cultures find it easier to organize and operate large corporations. Trust creates wealth.[36]

Trust is a valuable asset and needs to be carefully built-up and nurtured, also in small-scale cultures such as an innovation team, a project team or a management team.

Without [trust], engagement is minimized, creativity is stifled, and innovation is non-existent. With it, collaboration grows and high performance is attainable.[37]

Trust in Teams
The case for the centrality of trust in effective teams has been very simply argued:

---

[36]David Brooks: *The Social Animal*, 2011: 155.

[37]Roselyn Kay, "Trust as a Verb" in *Innovation Partners International Newsletter*, October 2010.

i. In the absence of trust team members are unwilling to be vulnerable and therefore do not engage in open conversations; they remain guarded.
ii. Where trust is low issues are discussed in a veiled manner and through guarded comments; there is caution about engaging fully and allowing all views to be fully aired; possible conflict is avoided.
iii. Where discussions are guarded and individuals do not feel able to air their views fully, when decisions are made they will inevitably lack the full commitment of all team members.
iv. Without commitment and buy-in team members will not hold themselves or each other accountable for the actions and behaviours, which the decisions were meant to produce.
v. Desired team results will be sacrificed for members' individual needs relating to ego, career development or recognition.[38]

Building the trust necessary to ensure the viability of departments, project teams and other groups begins with the individuals. Each person can take the initiative.

"Trust must be built one step at a time, by way of interpersonal confrontations and mutual engagements, by way of commitments and promises, offers and requests."[39] Again: "*Care* is perhaps the most essential ingredient of authentic trust, not only care about the immediate outcome but care about the relationship."[40]

---

[38]Patrick Lencioni, *The Five Dysfunctions of Teams*. 2002.

[39]Robert Solomon and Fernando Flores. *op.cit.*, Page 49

[40]*Ibid.* Page 105

Trust and Emotions

Trust is easily and very quickly damaged, through ignorance or carelessness. This is the case even when there appears to be a deep and solid foundation of trust, which it feels impossible to damage. Restoring trust, as with establishing authentic trust in the first place, requires:

- Courage;
- Absolute openness about oneself and to the other person (vulnerability);
- Time and patience;
- Avoiding assumptions about the other person and his or her motives;
- An open, enquiring frame of mind;
- Self-confidence, and an ability to trust oneself.

Following these guidelines is not easy. A felt breach of trust is almost inevitably accompanied by strong emotions like anger, outrage, remorse or sadness, and a tendency either to blame oneself or to blame the other person. When caught in an emotional storm it is impossible to display the openness, the curiosity, or the interest in the other person which rebuilding trust requires. To do so requires that full attention be paid to the other person.

In a genuine relationship, there is an outward flow of open, alert attention toward the other person.[41]

---

[41]Eckhart Tolle, *A New Earth*. 2005. Page 84

This is impossible when attention is directed inward, toward oneself and one's own negative thoughts and emotions. It does not mean that emotion should not be felt; it is part of the human experience. But it must not be allowed to become the driving force of one's subsequent actions.

Experimentation and Reflection

The following suggestions can help you to translate the material in this chapter to your own situation. They also offer opportunities to build trust or to restore trust which has been damaged.

- Think of a person whom you trust to a high degree. Think about *and write down* what it is about this person's behaviour, which has led you to develop this high degree of trust.
- Think of someone whose trust you would like to win. How might you create a conversation about the ideals and values that you might share?
- Think of a person whom you wish would trust you more. What specific things could you undertake in order to help build or create such trust?
- Trust is something extremely valuable. It is a huge pity if it disappears when that is not necessary. Think of someone you do not trust anymore. Are you certain that your interpretation of his actions is correct? How can you check whether you have not been guilty of jumping to premature conclusions?
- Think of a highly effective team. What contributed to the sense of mutual trust?

- If you wished to create more mutual trust in a team, what could you do?
- If someone has lost trust in you because of something you said or did, try to discuss with him or her what went wrong. Focus your attention on the other, not on your own feelings of regret, shame or guilt. Use Acknowledging as well as Asking and Listening behaviours.
- Think of initiatives you could take to *give* more trust to someone with whom you would like to develop a stronger relationship. Which behaviours will you need to use more, or more effectively?
- Think of a situation in which you experienced a breakdown of trust in an important relationship. What did you – or the other person – do in an attempt to restore the trust? Having read this chapter, what might you do differently on a next occasion?
- If you notice yourself becoming impatient because you feel you have invested enough to win back someone's trust, how could you force yourself to remain patient a while longer. Patience is of great importance. Trust is always slow to develop but quick to disappear. How could you discuss your own impatience with the other, without putting him or her under pressure?

4

FOUR LEVELS OF

COMMUNICATION

This sentense contains thre errors.

The statement above is peculiar. It contains two spelling errors, but the writer maintains that there are three errors. The third is an error on a different level: The sentence is not true, so it is an error at the level of meaning – it is just wrong. However, if we acknowledge that, then at the level of meaning the sentence is true again. This language trick makes clear that various levels can be referred to, such as spelling, sentence structure and meaning. When making a statement it is possible to make mistakes at different levels. In any communication there are always several levels at play simultaneously. That makes influencing others more complex than it might appear at first glance. In order to relate effectively to both the situation and your partner, it is necessary not only to be able to move flexibly from one dimension (*I, You* or *We*) to another, you also need to choose at which level you can best move forward.

When we say something, we not only convey a certain meaning at the level of content, we also engage in a relationship with the other, a relationship which in turn determines the meaning at the level of content. Gregory Bateson was the first to come upon this insight in the course of his research. He tried to uncover exactly what happens when a psychiatric patient speaks with family members. Does someone communicate strangely because he is a psychiatric patient, or does someone become a psychiatric patient because others, for example his parents, communicate in a strange and ambiguous manner? Paul Watzlawick translated Bateson's findings to communications in general. He identified a number of axioms which govern human communication, one of which states:

Every communication has a content and a relationship aspect such that the latter classifies the former and is therefore a meta-communication.[42]

When a mother says "Well done, son!" she expresses her appreciation for a successful action. At the same time she makes clear that she determines the standards by which her son will be judged and that her son is expected to live up to those standards. Every communicative expression carries with it different levels: what you say and the relationship which is created by saying it. Many attempts have been made to

[42]Paul Watzlawick, Janet H. Beavin and Don D. Jackson. *Pragmatics of Human Communication.* 1974. P.44

differentiate between levels of communication but in the context of organisational practice it is useful to distinguish between the following four levels:

Content: The topic or issue being addressed; all statements, questions, ideas, proposals, arguments etc. which deal with the subject at hand.

Procedure: The manner in which the issue is being discussed: sequence, timing, physical circumstances, agreements around responsibility and authority, and decision-making processes.

Interaction: The manner in which people deal with each other and respond to each other, for example: defensively, aggressively, considerately, cooperatively; whether the interaction is characterised by authoritarian tone-setting, a readiness to make mutual concessions, or submissiveness. This is frequently expressed non-verbally as well as in words: facial expression, body posture, distance, gestures, intonation, voice volume etc.

Climate: The mood which people are in during a discussion, the feelings which are contributing to a hopeful, high-energy atmosphere or a depressed, perhaps even tense climate. Even when they are not at the level of conscious awareness it's safe to say that everyone experiences certain feelings during a discussion. These feelings may be expressed directly with appropriate words, but they frequently find non-verbal expression.

FOUR LEVELS OF COMMUNICATION

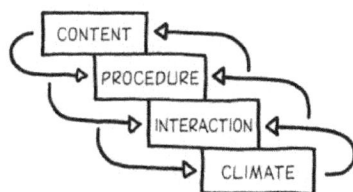

MOVE DOWN WHEN STUCK - THEN MOVE BACK UP

CONTENT: THAT WHICH IS BEING DISCUSSED
PROCEDURE: AGREEMENTS ABOUT HOW THE
                DISCUSSION WILL BE CONDUCTED
INTERACTION: THE WAY IN WHICH PARTICIPANTS ARE
                DISCUSSING AND REACTING TO EACH OTHER
CLIMATE: INDIVIDUALS' OR GROUP'S MOOD;
                THE LEVEL OF FEELINGS

We can look at another simple example:

A couple is seated in an automobile. The woman is behind the wheel; her husband is seated beside her. The car is waiting at a stoplight. At a certain moment the husband says: "The light is green."

With this remark the husband can express a number of different things. He could be stating merely an observation, namely that the light has jumped to green. But that is unlikely to be the only thing which he communicates. It may not even be the most important. He may be expressing his needs: "Come on, move! I don't want to be late." Alternatively, the statement may convey his opinion of his wife's driving: "You are not paying attention, again!"[43]

---

[43]F. Schulz von Thun: *Kommunizieren lernen (und umlernen)*. (Including the example) 1994

The simple sentence might mean a number of different things and depending on which meaning the wife responds to, the conversation can develop in any number of ways. She may respond with "Thank you", or: "Calm down, we'll make it in plenty of time" or: "Stop your eternal nagging about my driving; you're as bad as my father!"

The husband's words alone do not provide a clue regarding the message which he wishes to convey. He does not make his message explicit, for example by saying: "I have the impression that you're day-dreaming, because the light has been green for several seconds." It is easy to assume, as many of us do, that one or two words are enough. Those one or two words, however, are often very ambiguous in terms of meaning. Fortunately there are usually accompanying signals which facilitate the interpretation of the true meaning of the message, for example, the non-verbal signals (speaking quickly, impatiently or loudly, the facial expression) or the context in which they are spoken (the couple may be in danger of missing their flight). Nevertheless, misinterpretations and misunderstandings happen all too often: one person reacts to a message which the other had not intended. There is then a breakdown or disconnect in the communication. It is important to develop sensitivity for the different messages which could be wrapped into one verbal expression.

Look at an example from an organisational setting. Towards the end of a meeting someone says: "We don't have much time!"

This comment can be a pure observation of fact. More likely, it will point to procedural issues (*"Let's speed things up and keep a careful eye on the time."*), it may also express a feeling (*"I am getting impatient."*) or it can refer to a disturbing interactive pattern (*"We are all speaking at great length about this and starting to repeat ourselves."*). How do you interpret and respond to the statement? Do you start feeling rushed? Do you experience it as a reprimand? Do you see it as welcome support for the successful and timely completion of the meeting?

Content, Procedure, Interaction or Climate?

This distinction between the four levels can be very helpful, particularly when a conversation is in danger of derailing and there is a need to get it back on track. For example, imagine yourself in a difficult conversation with a colleague. Additional (scarce) resources for a key project are at stake. You make your wishes clear and start to discuss them. Initially the meeting moves forward in a business-like and rational fashion, but then the temperature suddenly rises. Your colleague suddenly bursts out with:

"Well, wait just a minute. You're putting a lot of pressure on me and I don't like it. So back off!"

How do you respond? How could or should you respond? The connection with the colleague is under threat. There is more at issue here than just choosing the right Dimension or the right behaviour within a Dimension with which to respond.

1. Do you concentrate on continuing the search for the most effective way to allocate available resources? (Content level)
2. Do you focus on the way the conversation is moving forward, on the steps which still need to be taken? (Procedure level)
3. Do you focus on the way in which the two of you are carrying out the discussion and reacting to each other? (Interaction level)

4. Or do you focus on how you and your colleague are experiencing the discussion and on the current climate? (level of Climate)

Depending on the level which you choose to address you can then deploy a wide range of influence behaviour. In response to your colleague's outburst you could, for example, respond with:

"That is not my intent. Let's just look at the issue again. It's difficult, but important so let's stay calm. I think we can probably free up Anton to work on my project."(*I-dimension*: Requesting, Declaring)

You have chosen to respond by trying to move ahead with the topic of your meeting, what you have come together to discuss in the first place. Your response is focused on the content being discussed. Alternatively, you could respond with something like:

"Is it okay with you if I first tell you clearly what's at stake here for me, and then let me try to understand where your priorities lie?"(*I-dimension*: Requesting)

You have chosen to respond with a suggestion as to how best to move forward from this point. You are trying to suggest a procedure which will help to ensure a positive outcome. You might, as a third alternative, try this:

"So you feel that I'm focusing too much on my own concerns here, not giving enough consideration to your priorities? Is that right?" (*You-dimension*: Listening)

This response steps back from further immediate discussion of the resource issue. You are focusing on the manner in which you and your colleague are behaving towards one another. You raise the issue of the pattern of interaction, which has become less than productive, threatening a breakdown of the discussion and a disconnect between you and the other person. A fourth alternative might be:

"I sense that you're really getting irritated with me. I think I can understand that, if I try to put myself in your position." (*You-dimension*: Listening, + *We-dimension*: Acknowledging) or:

"Your comment caught me off guard; I'm puzzled, and unsure how best to respond." (*We-dimension*: Sharing Feelings, Disclosing Needs)

These reactions focus on the climate which has been generated in the course of the exchange. In the first example you put into words which feeling you are picking up on in the other and letting the other know that you can understand how it might come that he feels that way. In the second example you put into words your own feelings of the moment. Both can be seen as attempts to reconnect at a human, relational level.

Focus on Task, Focus on Relationships

In the 1960s and early 1970s a number of leadership models were developed which highlighted the need for leaders to be aware of and work with two equally important focuses of attention. Going under various names ("Theory X and Theory Y"[44], "concern for production" and "concern for people"[45], "focus on task" and "focus on relationships"[46]) they all highlighted the necessity for leaders to look at their

---

[44]Douglas McGregor: *The Human Side of Enterprise*. 1960.

[45]Robert Blake and Jane Mouton: *The Managerial Grid*. 1964

[46]Paul Hersey and Kenneth Blanchard: *Management of Organizational Behaviour*. 1969

environment through a bi-focal lens, balancing attention to the task and attention to relationships.

Leaders needed to motivate and challenge their people to reach high levels of achievement. Success itself is an enormous motivator. On the other hand leaders needed to build positive relationships with their people and ensure that the levels of cooperation and teamwork were inspiring. People require a sense of being valued and of belonging. What was recommended decades ago is still relevant in today's organisations. Today's generation of professionals enjoys being challenged to achieve, but is also searching for membership in a meaningful work community. Both elements are important; in their absence people leave, burn out or become cynical.

This distinction between task and relationship is also useful when attempting to influence others. On the one hand you need to be task-oriented: a problem needs to be solved, a decision made or a goal achieved. On the other hand you do not wish to damage your relationship with the other. You want the other to cooperate with you fully and to feel involved. The four levels of communication are valuable in terms of clarifying this dual focus. The Content and Procedure levels clearly relate to *task*, while attention paid to Interaction and Climate can strengthen the *relationship*. In short:

Task: content and procedure

Relationships: interaction and climate

Experience shows that moving forward on the task level is almost impossible if there are blockages at the relationships level. In the example above, the colleague bursts out at the level of interaction. He feels threatened, and does not wish to be spoken to in that manner. The relationship is under threat. It is therefore imperative to continue at that level. Afterwards, room will be created to move forward again at the task level.

Meeting Breakdowns

Meetings, whether between two people or within a larger group, always take place with a formal or informal agenda, which outlines the reason for the get-together. Typically, a decision must be made or a problem must be solved. There is, inevitably, time pressure to deal with. The participants have, if all is well, prepared themselves thoroughly. They arrive armed with the necessary papers or with documents filed on notebook computers. They greet each other, perhaps take a cup of coffee, and then get to work. An overwhelming majority of the exchanges which follow relate to the decision or problem being discussed; a small number might relate to procedural issues. There is of course nothing wrong with this at all; as long as the meeting is proceeding smoothly the first priority is to achieve the outcome for which the meeting was called. Organisational meetings are about successful projects, implemented decisions, delivery of products and services, generated income.

Unfortunately, what frequently happens is that the participants struggle to move forward at the content level while any neutral observer would note that horns have been locked in what sounds and feels like a duel, that nobody is listening to what is being said, that tempers are fraying, or that the discussion keeps setting off at a tangent. As they leave the room, not having accomplished anything except perhaps agreeing when to meet again, participants can be heard muttering under their breath: "...bloody meetings!"

What is significant here is that the participants at the

meeting are unaware of the available opportunities to influence the situation at a level other than that of content. They can guide the procedure; they can correct or stimulate the prevailing patterns of interaction; they can open up the climate for discussion by expressing their own frustration or by acknowledging the feelings they sense in others. What we observe is that when people feel they cannot contribute usefully at the content level, or feel unsure of themselves because a meeting is threatening to get bogged down, they disconnect, remain silent and miss significant opportunities to make a difference.

We do not generally communicate sufficiently about our manner of communicating. It is important to be able to move down flexibly to an underlying level. A negative climate (individuals feel threatened, irritated or bored) leads to poor interaction (individuals stop listening, they focus only on what they want to say next, they stop participating altogether) which leads to a breakdown at the levels of procedure and content. How can you ensure that the meeting gets back on track?

Levels and Dimensions
Responding at the content level is something most people are comfortable with. But how can you make an intervention at one of the other levels? This can be done with behaviours drawn from any of the three dimensions.

The three-dimensional behavioural model and the *4-level* model now under consideration are entirely independent of one another. In other words, it would be wrong to assume, as some people initially do, that interventions at the Task or Procedure levels will be predominantly feature the *I-dimension*, or that interventions at the Interaction or Climate/Feelings level will be feature *You-dimension* and *We-dimension* behaviours. Below are a few examples:

Content Level:

- "Let's decide to..." (Requesting, *I-dimension*)
- "What do you mean when you say...?" (Asking, *You-dimension*)
- "I need help to work out..." (Disclosing Needs, *We-dimension*)

Procedure Level:

- "We shouldn't spend more than fifteen minutes on this." (Declaring, *I-dimension*)
- "You sound concerned that we are not focusing on the real issue here. Is that right?" (Listening, *You-dimension*)
- "I understand your concern. If I were in your role, I would be really worried about the available time as well." (Acknowledging, *We-dimension*)

Interaction Level:

- "I don't like the way you keep interrupting everyone." (Declaring, *I-dimension*)
- "Judging by your expression, it looks like you don't feel you're being listened to. Is that right?" (Listening, *You-dimension*)
- "I'm delighted that we are finally taking the time to really listen to and connect with each other." (Sharing Feelings, *We-dimension*)

Climate Level:

- "I'm really fed up with the tension which builds every time we talk about this subject, and I want us to clear the air – now!" (Declaring, Requesting, *I-dimension*)

- "How are you feeling about this meeting?" (Asking, *You-dimension*)
- "I sense that you are feeling really relieved, having said this." (Acknowledging, *We-dimension*)

Effective Switching

- Recognise the level on which your partner is communicating and get in step. Caution: the real message may be hidden behind the expressed words.
- If a meeting appears stuck, work to unblock the situation by moving down one level at a time until the source of the blockage is uncovered and dealt with: from content to procedures to interaction to climate. If it is obvious that there is a great deal of tension in the air, start from the bottom and work up: deal with issues related to climate first, then move up to interaction and procedures as necessary before resuming work on the content.
- Initiatives taken on the level of procedure provide reassurance and increase the sense of participation because they give the other person room to contribute.
- Initiatives taken on the level of interaction make it possible to examine the way in which parties are relating to each other. It's important to make comments descriptive and non-evaluative so that the other person can recognise what you're saying.
- Through initiatives taken at the level of feeling you can make your presence heard and felt. If your expression of your own feeling is clear and unambiguous it will stimulate the other person to pay more attention to you, to listen more openly.

- Initiatives at the level of climate can also serve to show that you recognise and respect the feelings of the other person. This will encourage and stimulate the other person.

Experimentation and Reflection

Recognising the Levels of Communication

During all communication each of the levels is present and represented. But sometimes one level is more explicit and obvious than the others. It is important to recognise this in order to be able to continue the discussion in a manner which connects with the previous speaker. Below you will find a number of statements. On which level is the speaker operating?

Bear in mind that the impact of a verbal statement is heavily influenced by the non-verbal behaviour which accompanies it. That may affect how you interpret the statement. For example, a sentence ending with a question mark may not be intended or received as a question. ("Do you still not get it?") So more than one answer may be possible, depending on how you imagine the volume, intonation and facial expression. At the end you will find some possible answers.

1. I'd like to suggest that we defer further discussion of this subject until our next meeting.
2. What I'm noticing now is that we seem to be interrupting each other a great deal.
3. Regarding the issue currently on the table, my preference would be that we...
4. How do you think we should proceed at this point?
5. John, you don't look very happy at the moment. Is

something bothering you that you would like to say something about?

6. Let me try to understand what you're proposing. If I have understood you, your idea is that we basically need to rethink our strategy on this issue. Is that right?

7. I can imagine that you feel under attack now, and would like to defend yourself.

8. Fellows, I'm frankly very worried right now, and that's getting in the way for me.

If you now look at the dimensions of the Influence Model, which of the nine behaviours are being used here?

- *I-dimension*: Requesting, Reasoning, Promising, Declaring
- *You-dimension*: Asking, Listening
- *We-dimension*: Acknowledging, Sharing Feelings, Disclosing Needs

Possible answers:
- Procedure (Requesting)
- Interaction (Reasoning)
- Content (Requesting)
- Procedure (Asking)
- Climate (Asking)
- Content (Listening)
- Interaction (Acknowledging)
- Climate (Sharing Feelings)

Responding Flexibly from each Level of Communication

In principle we always have a choice regarding how we respond to someone else: from which Level of Communication we will next speak. This does not imply that each Level will be equally appropriate at every juncture in a discussion. But we do have a choice, and in order to make the best choice and respond in the most appropriate manner we need to develop flexibility.

Imagine someone saying each of the following things to you. Write down how you could respond at each Level of Communication:

Of course, while responding at or from a certain level you will also be using one of the nine Behaviours. Which Behaviour did you use? Afterwards, compare your answers with the ones we have suggested.

1. I think you're missing the point entirely here. You don't seem to have understood the seriousness of the problem.

2. I'm getting really tired of the way things have been going recently. We're just not moving forwards and it feels like we're all stuck somewhere.

3. I'm really extremely rushed at the moment; I'm under a lot of pressure. I don't see how I can help you with that report. Sorry!

4. You are absolutely wrong in your assessment of the situation! You really need to think things through more carefully before making a proposal.

5. It is a difficult client and I'd like you to make time in your agenda to handle the account from now on. This has a high priority for our department.

6. We need to reorganise our priorities. I think we should put less energy into client X and focus ourselves on creating a better long-term market strategy.

For possible answers see pages 124-126

Using the Four Levels of Communication

Recall a recent meeting in which you and the other participants were stuck; the discussion was going around in circles and not moving forward,

What did you do at the time? How constructive was that?

Now think of interventions (statements or questions) which you *could* have made. Write down four possible interventions, one each at the levels of:

- Content
- Procedure
- Interaction
- Feelings

Which one feels right as you think back to what was going on at the time? Imagine making the statement or asking the question. How do you imagine the other person(s) reacting? What could you do next?

Now resolve to try to do something different the next time you are in a similar setting where progress towards the meeting's objectives feels blocked. Experiment, and request feedback from a trusted colleague.

Possible answers to questions on p.123:

1. **Content**: "Yes, I have understood. And the point is…" (Declaring)

   Procedure: "I have obviously missed something, in your view. How you are looking at this problem? (Asking)

   Interaction: "Let's slow things down a bit and take more time to listen to each other." (Requesting)

   Climate: "You're starting to sound pretty upset and, quite

honestly, I'm hurt by what you just said." (Listening +
Sharing Feelings)

2. **Content**: "Complicated issues like this require a lot of
thinking!" (Declaring)
Procedure: "Okay, well, let's take some time now to talk
about how we're all feeling right now." (Requesting)
Interaction: "Do you feel we are just waiting for the
other guy to do something?" (Listening)
Climate: "Thank you for being open about this. I can
understand that you must be quite fed up right now."
(Acknowledging)

3. **Content**: "But I really do need your help! It's important!"
(Requesting)
Procedure: "Tell me what this pressure is all about; then
I'll tell you what makes this report so important. Let's see
if we reach an agreement that way." (Requesting)
Interaction: "It feels to me like at the moment we're not
really prepared to listen to each other. What's your sense
on this?" (Reasoning, Asking)
Climate: "You're sounding really worried and stressed
out. What's this about?" (Listening, Asking)

4. **Content**: "Okay, please help me to understand what I'm
missing here." (Asking)
Procedure: "Let me tell you how I reached my
assessment; then I'd like you to tell me what you feel I
missed." (Requesting)
Interaction: "I wonder if it's going to help if we start bad-
mouthing each other. Let's try again to listen carefully."
(Declaring)
Climate: "That hurts me, and I'm really puzzled as to why

you are taking such a strong stand on this." (Sharing Feelings, implied Asking)

5. **Content**: "Thank you! That is the sort of challenge I've been looking for!" (Declaring)

   Procedure: "I'd appreciate it if you could tell me exactly what you expect of me first; then we can discuss whether I'm going to be the right person for this." (Requesting)

   Interaction: "You have caught me off guard on this one. It would help me if you explained your thinking before pressing me for a decision." (Declaring, Requesting)

   Climate: "I'm really feeling excited by this chance! Also a bit worried, to be quite honest. But you sound like you're under a lot of pressure at the moment. What's going on?" (Sharing Feelings, Listening, Asking)

6. **Content**: "I believe you could be making a mistake by discounting Client X. Recent trends with that client – and with that market in general – have shown that we could be on the verge of a major upsurge in demand. Here, let me show you..." (Reasoning)

   Procedure: "Before we make a decision on this, let's look carefully at what our recent history with X has been, and see if we can weigh off the advantages and disadvantages of following your suggestion." (Requesting)

   Interaction: "You seem to reach these conclusions without really consulting any of the rest of us beforehand. I'd appreciate it if you involve us at an early stage, instead of confronting us like this." (Declaring, Requesting)

   Climate: "I'm really disappointed with this statement, after all the work I've put into X. I'm also confused about why you're coming with this at this time." (Sharing Feelings)

5

COMMUNICATING

WITHOUT WORDS

Creating and maintaining connection during a conversation is always challenging. It requires flexibility in terms of the three dimensions and the four levels. But that is not the end of it. A third aspect plays a vital role: conscious and unconscious behaviour, verbal and non-verbal communication. In order to understand another's meaning or intention you do not just listen to the words, but also to the non-verbal signals. Is the remark "It's warm in here" simply information, a call to action, or a reprimand? Intonation, volume and facial expression will determine what the meaning is, whether these are intended or unintended, conscious or unconscious. Think of any recent discussion you took part in or presentation you made. What comes to mind first? Probably the place where you were sitting or standing, the facial expression or other non-verbal responses of the other. Verbal comments which come to mind will also be coupled with recollections of the non-verbal signals from the other. That is what leaves an indelible memory.

Do not underestimate how much professional speakers practice their use of voice and body. Before going on-stage guest speakers or talk-show hosts often do exercises to loosen up their voice (breathing, exaggerated articulation, humming from low tones to high and back again) and to loosen up their bodies (stretching, shaking, tightening and relaxing muscles). It is really remarkable how often we begin a discussion without ensuring that our voice and body are prepared. No wonder we sometimes come across as stiff and monotone.

When working with voice and body you can focus on a number of different aspects.

Voice:

- Articulation: careful, precise, or nonchalant, relaxed;
- Volume: loud or soft;
- Tone: high or low;
- Tempo: slow or quick;
- Continuing to talk or letting silences fall (also before or after your contribution).

Body:

- Position in relation to the other: close, distant, higher, lower;
- Sitting or standing;
- Movement: walking, standing still, using available space;
- Gestures: many or few, large or small;
- Facial expression: stern or serious, smiling or relaxed;
- Eye contact.

People are very sensitive to the way they experience someone's presence. Think of the kinds of things they say if asked to comment on someone's contribution: "He seemed very relaxed", "Her enthusiasm was obvious", or "If you ask me he was quite irritated". How did we develop this high degree of sensitivity for the non-verbal aspect of behaviour? Words are frequently very ambiguous in their meaning. "Ball" can refer to a round object for throwing, hitting or kicking, a festive gala occasion marked by dancing and fancy dress, or in American slang to a good time, as in "We had a ball!". This ambiguity is even more true of complete sentences. In order to determine just what someone means, it is necessary to pay attention to the non-verbal signals as well as to the verbal content of the message. Do you interpret the remark "The scope of your report is more restricted than we had expected" as a neutral comment, an incentive, a compliment or a criticism? Emphases, intonation, volume, facial expression and gestures provide the keys to accurate interpretation.

We are particularly sensitive to any lack of congruence between verbal and non-verbal behaviour. If someone says to you that you have his full attention and that he has all the time in the world for you, while looking around in all directions or glancing at his watch, then this non-verbal behaviour will give you an unpleasant feeling, because the words do not impress as being sincere. When verbal and non-verbal behaviour are not congruent then our interpretation of the intended meaning relies for only 7% on the spoken word and for 93% on non-verbal behaviour (38% voice, 55% body language).[47]

---

[47]Albert Mehrabian: *Silent Messages*, 1972.

Why are we so sensitive to non-verbal behaviour? This is because we rely first on our feelings and only secondly on our thinking. That is not as strange as it may sound, because our brain is driven in the first instance by feelings and impulses.

Feeling and Thinking

Expressed behaviour has two sources: our thoughts and our feelings. Of these two sources, feelings are by far the most important in terms of their impact on human interaction and on the quality of the connection which is made between individuals.

This statement apparently contradicts the notion embedded in the term *homo sapiens*, meaning "wise human" or "knowing human". We take pride in being the only species on the planet capable of abstract reasoning, language, introspection and problem solving. Though we possess a very highly developed part of the brain called the neo-cortex, the base of the human brain, the amygdala, is in fact very primitive. It is the source of emotional responses, which are triggered much more quickly than considered, thoughtful responses.[48]

Human behaviour is typically marked by great inconsistencies which originate in the on-going struggle between the different parts of the brain. Though these parts work together, they also operate independently and the oldest part is dominant in terms of triggering instantaneous emotional responses. This reptilian brain is programmed to

---

[48]Daniel Goleman, Chapter 2 ("Anatomy of an Emotional Hijacking") of *Emotional Intelligence*, 1995. Goleman provides an informative and readable overview of the structure and operation of the human brain.

eat, sleep, procreate, fight or flee, and constitutes the deepest levels of our own mental software. When people say that they were "beside themselves" or excuse themselves with "I don't know what got into me" they usually refer to an instance in which an emotional and irrational response to a situation was triggered. The rational part of the brain did not have time to intervene and plan a more considered, appropriate response. The outer brain, the neo-cortex can be seen as a sort of social layer, which enables planning and collaboration with others, tempering or regulating emotional responses – but also rationalising after the fact, formulating a justification for explosive behaviour.

Verbal and Non-Verbal Behaviour

Though feelings play a dominant role in terms of driving human behaviour we are seldom aware of this, certainly not in the business environment. We prefer to harbour the illusion that we are fully in control, operating from our rational control centre. Therefore we tend to pay the greatest attention to verbal behaviour, that which we express with words. This, in turn, leads to an incomplete picture of the means whereby we can and do communicate and influence others. For the most part we express our emotions non-verbally, through our body language and voice rather than with words. And the non-verbal part of behaviour invariably has significant impact. An example:

It was in the Vietnam War, and an American platoon was hunkered down in some rice paddies, in the heat of a fire-fight with the Vietcong. Suddenly a line of six monks started walking along the elevated berms that separated paddy from paddy. Perfectly calm and poised, the monks walked directly towards the line of fire.

"They didn't look right, they didn't look left. They walked straight through," recalls David Busch, one of the American soldiers. "It was really strange, because nobody shot at 'em. And after they walked over the berm, suddenly all the fight was out of me. I just didn't feel I wanted to do this anymore, at least not that day. It must have been that way for everybody, because everybody quit. We just stopped fighting."[49]

Feelings are extraordinarily contagious. The example above is one of positive contagion: the inner calm of the monks dissipated the soldiers' will to fight. We also see frequent examples of negative contagion: our own irritation or anger calls forth similar feelings in others, even before we can take note of the fact. We tend to blame others for showing irritation, quite unaware of the fact that we have triggered it ourselves through our own non-verbal behaviour. It works the other way around as well of course: we will respond to another person based on his or her underlying feelings as expressed, even if it is very subtly, through body posture, facial expression, or the eyes, once again without even being aware of it. Try looking in the mirror some day when you have been with people who were in a bad mood!

This is of great importance for the way in which we seek to influence others. We need to become more aware of the manner

---

[49]Daniel Goleman, *op.cit.*, page 114

in which we are ourselves influenced by the emotions of others. If we do not, then our emotional brain (the amygdala) will take us for a ride every time. We are then not consciously occupied in influencing others, but are responding (unconsciously) to the threat or temptation of the other. (Remember: "influence" has the same etymological roots as "influenza", a disease which arrives unnoticed.) In summary our behaviour is not driven in the first instance by the two sources, thinking and feeling, but by the preceding step: our largely emotional and unconscious responses to the behaviour of others. In other words, in the drawing below, it is important to realise that *our feelings, emotions* are to a large extent triggered as unconscious responses to others.

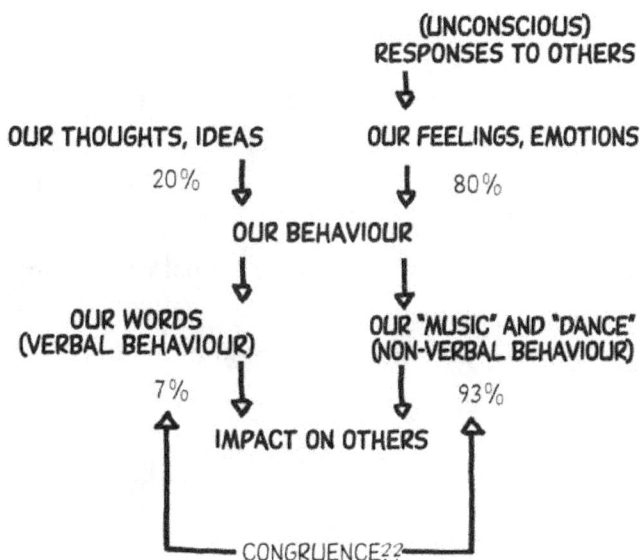

**(UNCONSCIOUS)
RESPONSES TO OTHERS**
↓

OUR THOUGHTS, IDEAS   **OUR FEELINGS, EMOTIONS**
20% ↓   ↓ 80%

OUR BEHAVIOUR
↓

**OUR WORDS
(VERBAL BEHAVIOUR)**   **OUR "MUSIC" AND "DANCE"
(NON-VERBAL BEHAVIOUR)**
7% ↓   ↓ 93%

IMPACT ON OTHERS

CONGRUENCE??

Listening to signals from your body

Emotions are contagious and we are very susceptible to them. We possess very sensitive antennae. Sensing emotions carried in a face is easier for our brains than identifying them. Researchers at Princeton University discovered that the emotional centre has completed its task within a hundred milliseconds of the appearance of an image on the retina. The rational brain is simply too late to impact on the emotional judgment with a rational consideration of what we know or can assume about someone. In addition, faces with an emotional expression have priority in the brain. Shy individuals, who in strange company tend to put on a neutral expression, are often literally overlooked.

The challenge is to make these received signals available to our awareness. A good medium for this is your own body awareness. Learn to pick up on the signals which your body is giving you: is it getting more tense or more relaxed? Does it crave something or does it want to get as far away as possible? Imitation of the behaviour of others is also a clear sign of influence. Sometimes we notice that we are starting to imitate another person in terms of posture or the use of voice: leaning backwards, crossing the legs, speaking more quickly or more slowly. The human tendency to imitate is very strong, especially when it concerns people who are fond of each other. People who spend a great deal of time together start to resemble each other. During one study photographs of men and women were shown to subjects with the question, who is married to whom? The partners were often clearly recognised, because facial expressions tend to become increasingly similar in the course of years. Partners who get on well with each other and have been together for a long time, tend to use the same facial muscles, and similar lines start to show on their faces.

When another person starts to imitate your non-verbal signals then there is contact and openness. You can also use this fact actively. Imitating another person can be to your advantage. A study showed that waiters who imitated their clients, for example by repeating the order back, received significantly higher tips.

All this is valid in all cultures; however each culture has its own repertoire of appropriate and inappropriate non-verbal behaviour for any given situation. On the other hand, it has been found that facial expressions indicating anger, disgust, fear, joy, sadness and surprise are almost universal. But it takes a great deal of effort to understand and interpret other non-verbal signals in a different culture accurately. Avoiding eye contact can be a sign of respect – or the opposite. Shaking of the head can mean "no" in one culture, and "yes" in another.

Working on Non-Verbal Behaviour

Is it possible to work on effective non-verbal behaviour if so much of it is unconscious? Fortunately it is. We are, for the most part unconsciously, keenly sensitive to the feelings which we pick-up on through the behaviour of others. The challenge is to gain access to your unconscious. For this we need to rely on intuition:

A person watching a two-second video clip of a teacher he or she has never met will reach conclusions about how good that teacher is that are very similar to those of a student who has sat in on the teacher's class for an entire semester.[50]

---

[50]Malcolm Gladwell: Blink: *The Power of Thinking Without Thinking*, 2005. 13

Very quickly, in two seconds, even without sound, we have a pretty good impression of someone, and others of us, of course. In order to learn about our own non-verbal behaviour we need only invite others to share their first impressions. But that doesn't happen easily. The others must be able to observe your behaviour well; they need to be able to rely on their intuition; they must be able to express their intuition in understandable language; and they need to feel safe enough to tell you what their first impressions are. Finally, of course, you need to be open to hear what they say. This can be achieved in the personal or work environment among individuals who are positively disposed towards each other. Receiving honest feedback concerning your behaviour is an extremely useful method of self-analysis.

Socrates was only partly right when he stated that the "unexamined life is not worth living". The key is the kind of self-examination people perform, and the extent to which people attempt to know themselves solely by looking inward, versus looking outward at their own behaviour and how others react to them.[51]

In addition it is important to observe your own instinctive responses to the behaviour of others. We have referred to this before. How aware are you of your physical reactions? What does your body and your voice then express? Simply paying attention to it regularly can also help in developing this sensitivity. For example, you can ask yourself five times a day: what am I feeling right now? Realise too that you are often experiencing several feelings at once (a little tired, curious, uncertain...)

---

[51]Timothy D. Wilson: *Strangers to Ourselves*, 2002. 16

It is important to observe yourself constantly, though this is not always easy. In difficult situations we are absorbed in our behaviour and our conscious awareness is restricted. Begin by observing how people respond (non-verbally) to others. Then gradually try to participate while observing yourself carefully. How do you say things and what is the (non-verbal) response of others? This is the way actors learn: reciting a text and simultaneously listening to the colour and power of their voice.

To get a good sense for your use of voice and body language it is best to experiment with a (video) recording device. Try whatever comes to mind. Feel how it sounds, what your body is expressing. Experience the impact.

Another powerful way of learning is to observe famous examples. On *You-Tube* you can for example watch and listen to Barack Obama or other well-known contemporary speakers. On television you can observe good interviewers at work. You can purchase DVDs with endless examples of powerful communication in movies. A good example can be very inspiring. Athletes learn a great deal by studying in detail the movements of their role models or heroes. Athletes prepare themselves mentally before a competition. They see themselves doing it; they see themselves winning. It helps. It's called *priming* in psychological jargon. A study showed that individuals who spent five minutes freely associating around words like "professor" and "university" prior to starting a game of Trivial Pursuit scored significantly higher than people who did not do this. While preparing yourself for a difficult discussion it is useful to put yourself in the place of someone whom you have seen carry on this type of discussion effectively.

By regularly using different non-verbal behaviour consciously it will gradually embed itself in your unconscious repertoire, just as a piano player files away well-practiced runs in his reptilian brain and can later play them as if on autopilot.

Our habits do not stem from our character, but our character from our habits.

Aristotle

Non-verbal behaviour is also powerful and important in the workplace. Therefore:

It might be a good idea to cut down on the tele-conferences and work harder to get people face-to-face. Most communication is physical – through gestures not words. It's hard to understand others or share ideas and plans across a video screen.[52]

Non-Verbal Behaviour and the Three Dimensions

What are the consequences of these considerations for the application of the influence model? Below you will find a number of tips regarding the non-verbal aspects of the three dimensions.

I-dimension

- Be concise.
- Speak with a firm, quiet voice; don't end a sentence on a higher tone (sounds like a question!), maintain your volume.
- Maintain direct eye-contact throughout, and for a second or two when you have finished speaking.

---

[52]David Brooks: *The Social Animal,* 2011. 240

- Use appropriate (firm) gestures in order to emphasise points.
- Sit or stand straight when speaking.

Focus on and feel your strong conviction or sense of indignation, so that energy from within is released.

You-dimension
- Facial expression and body posture convey authentic interest or curiosity.
- Maintain eye-contact when the other is speaking.
- Permit silences when the other needs time to think.
- Adapt the speed and intensity of your speaking to match the other.
- Mirror the posture and gestures of the other with your own body

You need to be authentically interested or curious!

We-dimension
- Bend slightly towards the other person.
- Take the time to think about what the other has said before responding.
- Demonstrate vulnerability by speaking in a slightly hesitant, considered way.
- Don't stare at the other; allow your eyes to drift occasionally.
- Speak authentically, from the heart.

Behaviour in this dimension comes over best if you are really moved. You can be moved if you can really empathise with the other, and also allow yourself to experience your own feelings fully.

Controlling Inappropriate Non-Verbal Behaviour

Even if you master all the skills required to influence others, things can go wrong. You don't have the desired impact because disturbing feelings get in your way: you're afraid you won't succeed anyway, you shrink back from a possible confrontation or you are irritated and impatient. As a result of these feelings your *I-dimension* behaviour is weak, you can't listen with attention and interest, or you come across as distant or aloof. The problem is that these feelings will find expression in your non-verbal behaviour (you speak hesitantly, you smile inappropriately, your eyes wander). The other will pick up the signals and respond – for the most part unconsciously – to them. In this way you may find yourself confirmed in what you were afraid of in the first place.

It is possible to come to grips with this and to restrict inappropriate non-verbal behaviour. This is done by making a careful analysis of the convictions and assumptions which guide your speaking. Becoming aware of unexpressed thoughts and feelings, understanding where they come from and why you don't express them can provide new openings towards an effective discussion.

What follows is an example of such an analysis: the *left-hand column analysis*. The right hand column contains the most important things you actually said. The left-hand column contains the unexpressed thoughts and feelings. The context in this example concerns a consultant's discussion with a client after delivering a successful training programme to the client organisation.

What I thought and felt but did not express:	**What was said:**
Feel: proud	Client: That was an excellent programme again!
	I: Yes, it went really well.
Think: That's good for my turnover Think: Where is this going? Feel: unsure	Client: We are planning a new one for the autumn. Say, do you remember Charles, not from this group but the one before that?
	I: uh …
Feel: sympathy for Charles Think: What does she really want?	Client: The tall, blond guy from R&D?
	I: Oh yes. We had an intensive one-on-one during the programme.
Think: Oh oh! There we go! Feel: Anxiety	Client: He was very moved by his whole experience and would like some follow up sessions.
Think: How am I going to fit this in? She's saddling me with a problem. Sounds like she promised him something.	I: That's good to hear, but my agenda is really full at the moment.

Feel: worried (that she finds
me uninterested)

Think: Don't be so pushy. She's not hearing me. Feel: Irritation	Client: But he really wants to pursue this with you, and you have coached others successfully in the past as well.
Think: I can only coach well if I have sufficient rest and peace, not crammed between other things Think: she's put a knife to my throat now Feel: indignation Think: I'm going to lose this Feel: discouraged	I: Okay, but my agenda is completely full for the next two months. Client: That's too long; the training will have lost its effect then. Suppose you just agree to a first meeting with him.
	I: Okay, that should be possible. But he has to understand that there will be a lengthy gap before a next session.
Think: This is going much too fast. *You* should tell him Feel: irritation	Client: Sure, you can just tell him that. Shall I tell him that he can drop by next week?

Think: What a sucker I am!
How am I going to explain   I: Okay, let's give it a try.
this at home?
Feel: Weak
Think: I'm such a failure, I
can't even conduct my own
conversations convincingly!

The end result of this conversation is, as we see, that the consultant cannot influence the client to respond to coaching requests more carefully.

If you examine the left-hand column you will see that there are many feelings and thoughts which were left unexpressed. But they probably did come through to the client non-verbally: hesitant speech, uncomfortable posture, sighing, looking down, speaking softly. The left-hand column leaks into the right.

It is theoretically possible to practice hiding all those non-verbal signals and replacing them with more appropriate behaviour. But the real problem lies elsewhere: apparently there are blocks which ensure that you don't make some of your feelings explicit. In the influence model the *We-dimension* suggests a way of sharing feelings and disclosing underlying needs. By doing so, your verbal behaviour becomes congruent with your non-verbal behaviour, which will enhance the impact of the whole. It is worth discovering what the blocks are and clearing them away. But take note: it is not necessary that you blurt out everything which ends up in the left-hand column during a discussion! The important question is: why do you choose to make some things explicit and some not? Are the assumptions you make justified?

From several elements in the left-hand column the consultant could identify the following assumptions:

- I feel proud, but I don't disclose that. Apparently I believe it's not okay to boast. In this way I miss a chance to show my enthusiasm.
- I feel unsure about the direction the conversation seems to be taking, but say nothing. Apparently I believe that as a professional you have to demonstrate self-assurance. I miss a chance to build a warm relationship with her.
- I think the client has promised Charles something but I fail to check that out. Apparently I believe that it's not done to ask unnecessary questions. I miss the opportunity to understand the client's drivers fully.
- I think I am going to lose. Apparently I see a discussion as a fight with a winner and a loser. In this way I miss a possibility to see this as an attempt to help me, for example by giving me more billable hours.
- I feel irritated and angry but don't say so. Apparently I assume that it's not okay to have an argument with a client. In this way I fail to protect myself by ensuring I have sufficient rest and time to coach effectively.

These assumptions need to be critically examined. Which are valid, and which need to be seriously challenged. The consultant might decide that, the next time, he will:

- Permit himself to show more enthusiasm.
- Be open about any feelings of uncertainty about the direction of a conversation. Or

- Be open and frank with a client; disagreements are okay!

The result will be a greater degree of congruence between what is said and what is felt. This in turn will result in a stronger impact than the distant, "professional" approach of the consultant in the example.

Appropriate use of all three dimensions can help to break down the influence of disturbing feelings:

- *You-dimension*: avoid jumping to conclusions, paraphrase what you think the other meant and if necessary ask clarifying questions. Check whether you are reading the feelings of the other person correctly.
- *I-dimension*: Express the conclusions you draw and the judgments you make clearly and directly, and be honest about what you want.
- *We-dimension*: be open about your own feelings, concerns and doubts; try to see things from the other's perspective and confirm the legitimacy of doubts, concerns and feelings which you pick up on from the other.

Create a climate of trust, openness, understanding and mutual respect, within which a spirit of harmonious cooperation can be forged.

Experimentation and Reflection

Observing and interpreting non-verbal behaviour

Television soap operas can provide a daily exercise in reading non-verbal behaviour. Turn off the sound and look exclusively at the gestures and facial expressions of the actors. Note specific actions and expressions in as much detail as possible. What do you think is going on? The chances are high that you will understand the interpersonal dynamics being portrayed with a high degree of accuracy.

The public arena (on the street, in restaurants and so on) always provides an on-going theatre in which to observe human behaviour. Try to establish what kind of mood people are in by looking at how they carry themselves when they stand, sit or walk. Look at a couple sitting at a table in a restaurant: by observing their glances, gestures and expressions try to establish what the nature or quality of their relationship is. People-watching is a favourite pastime for many.

Make a point of observing people in your work environment carefully. Find opportunities where it is not essential that you focus on the words and where you are free to direct your attention entirely to the other person's voice and his or her body language. How are they feeling about being there? How do they feel about the discussion in which they are taking part?

You can do these things by yourself but it is more fun to do together with someone else, and checking and comparing your observations. This helps you to learn about non-verbal behaviour in a playful manner. Once you have practiced a bit you can apply your new skills during business meetings.

Observing your own non-verbal behaviour

Once you have sensitised yourself to non-verbal behaviour by watching others, turn the tables on yourself. Which idiosyncratic gestures, facial expressions and uses of voice can you notice in yourself? How do these reflect your moods? How might others interpret these signals? Ask others what they notice about you and how they interpret your behaviours.

If possible, for example with a Smartphone which has a video function, record yourself or ask someone to record you. Listen and watch critically. What do you like, what might have a negative effect? What can you change?

Experimenting with non-verbal behaviour
Once again, if possible record your experimentation for later review.

Articulation

Clear articulation is important in order to be understood. So-called tongue-twisters offer a light-hearted way of practicing this skill. Many more can be found on the internet. Trying reading them out loud, starting slowly and then speeding up.

- A box of biscuits, a batch of mixed biscuits
- Sam's shop stocks short spotted socks
- We surely shall see the sun shine soon
- She sells sea shells by the sea shore.
  The shells she sells are surely seashells.
  So if she sells shells on the seashore,
  I'm sure she sells seashore shells.
- I am not the pheasant plucker,
  I'm the pheasant plucker's mate.
  I am only plucking pheasants
  'cause the pheasant plucker's late.

Voice and Gestures

Several texts are provided below for you to experiment with. Children's stories are also very useful – imagine yourself reading the story to a child, and making the reading as dramatic as possible, using your voice and your body to gain maximum effect. Use whatever text appeals to you, and look for poems in your own language if necessary. While reading, experiment and look for things which work for you even if they feel strange and therefore uncomfortable at first. If you record your efforts you will probably discover that your non-verbal behaviour was less exaggerated than you first thought. There is a big difference between how we see ourselves, and how others see us.

Amelia Mixed the Mustard (A.E. Housman)

> Amelia mixed the mustard,
> She mixed it good and thick;
> She put it in the custard
> And made her Mother sick,
> And showing satisfaction
> By many a loud huzza,
> "Observe," she said, "the action
> Of mustard on Mamma."

Epigram (Jonathan Swift)

As Thomas was cudgelled one day by his wife,
He took to the street, and fled for his life:
Tom's three dearest friends came by in the squabble,
And saved him at once from the shrew and the rabble;
Then ventured to give him some sober advice –
But Tom is a person of honour so nice,
Too wise to take counsel, too proud to take warning,
That he sent to all three a challenge next morning.
Three duels he fought, thrice ventured his life;
Went home, and was cudgelled again by his wife.

The Lake Isle of Innisfree (William Butler Yeats)

I will arise and go now, and go to Innisfree,
And a small cabin build there, of clay and wattles
    made:
Nine bean-rows will I have there, and a hive for the
    honey-bee,
And live alone in the bee-loud glade.

And I shall have some peace there, for peace comes
    dropping slow,
Dropping from the veils of the morning to where the
    cricket sings;
There midnight's all a glimmer, and noon a purple
    glow,
And evening full of the linnet's wings.

I will arise and go now, for always night and day
I hear lake water lapping with low sounds by the
    shore;
While I stand on the roadway, or on the pavements
    grey,
I hear it in the deep heart's core.

A short address to a business meeting
*This is a business address with different twists and turns
(serious, stern, enthusiastic, motivating). Try to
emphasise each of these moods. Permit silences, pause.
Exaggerate!*

What I have to tell you now is very important. If we do
not make the changes outlined in this report, it is not
just our productivity that will suffer. The respect for
our brand, the security of our jobs, the welfare of our
dependents – all will be placed in jeopardy. The time
has passed when we could sit back and congratulate
ourselves on being a successful company. What we have
experienced since the beginning of the year is a
catalogue of disasters. Now we have the power to say –
yes, things have gone wrong, but we can change this.
We are fighting for our lives, but we have a new
awareness, a vibrant energy and a crystal clear
determination – we shall win through.

A news report (Timesonline.co.uk, April 14th 2008)
*(Read this first as if it were just another dry piece of
business news; read it soberly and without any emotion.*

Then read it again as if it were the most astonishing or alarming news of the day, as if you can hardly contain yourself whilst reading! Alternatively, read any current news-article in your local newspaper.)

CITIGROUP and Merrill Lynch will heap further pain on Wall Street this week as they reveal additional sub-prime write-downs totalling $15 billion (£7.6 billion) or more.

In another sign of the intense pressure on leading banks, Deutsche Bank is attempting to offload some of its €35 billion (£28 billion) of toxic debt to a consortium of private-equity firms.

Huge exposure to American mortgages is expected to result in Citi taking a $10 billion hit to its accounts, dragging the bank to a first-quarter loss of almost $3 billion. Some analysts believe Citi's write-downs could stretch to as much as $12 billion.

Merrill will suffer $5 billion of write-downs, analysts say, which would push the bank $2.7 billion into the red.

The Left-Hand Column Analysis

Create your own right – and left-hand analysis, based on a recent discussion you had. See the example on pages 141-143.
- Recall a difficult discussion you engaged in recently.
- Take a blank piece of paper and draw a vertical line down the middle.
- Use the right-hand column to record, as best you can, the actual words you and the other spoke during a part of the discussion.

- Note down unexpressed thoughts and feelings you had in the left-hand column.
- Is it obvious that there are certain feelings and thoughts which you keep to yourself?
- Which assumptions do you appear to be making – assumptions about yourself, about the other person or about the situation?
- Are these assumptions really justified in this situation?
- What did you lose in this discussion as a result of your assumptions?
- How could you adjust or change these assumptions?

AFTERWORD

In this book we have described the concepts we use when training individuals to lead more influential discussions. We have included sections on *Experimenting and Reflecting* in each chapter to help you familiarise yourself with different forms of behaviour. The question remains, however, whether true learning is fundamentally about theories and skills practice at all. Some time ago we analysed evaluation forms completed by 268 participants who had done one version or another of the programme *Focus on Influence*. A few of their responses follow:

- Helped me to accept myself and get to know myself better.
- Very reflective in the sense that I thought about "Who am I?" and got a lot of surprising feedback that had impact to that question.
- Revealing experience in terms of learning to create trust; strong emotional impact.
- I have learned how to involve emotions in my work and I realised that it is more important than I could ever imagine.
- Eye-opener on the complexity of human interaction.
- Difficult and challenging journey.
- Transformational, a kind of spiritual experience towards the end.
- I have seen and done some beautiful things.

Two of the most poignant comments were the following:
"I actually found myself even though I did not know that I was lost," and "Really helped me to regain faith in myself." These seem to indicate that our "behavioural laboratory" has more than a clinical effect on improving the effectiveness of behaviour; that a deeper layer around self-awareness and self-realisation also gets addressed. In order to effect real changes in behaviour and attitude it is likely that something must change, or be rediscovered, at this layer. Otherwise newly found skills threaten to get washed away quickly in the stream of every-day events and experiences. We hope that this book will speak to the reader's deeper layers as well.

From a point of view of programme design, it is not the brilliance of the concepts, the clarity of the facilitators' presentations and the carefully thought-out exercises which, in the end, generate these types of responses. Though they are necessary, it is the total mix of the event, including the group, the facilitators, and the venue which, together, create the environment in which profound learning can take place. We are always struck by how frequently the group gives itself credit for the learning achieved: the openness, the trust, the interest in hearing of each others' experiences and the candid one-on-one conversations.

In order to get the most out of this book it is wise to enter into conversations with others whom you trust and who know you well, about the insights and questions this book has raised. Such conversations can help you to focus your attention on what really matters when it comes to enhancing the effectiveness of your influence behaviour.

Shifting Learning Goals

At the start of a programme we always ask participants to say, in a few words, what the learning goals are which they have brought with them. The range of answers is obviously enormous, but it is safe to say that the majority fall within the range of what in our model we call *I-dimension* behaviours. On the final evaluation form we asked participants to indicate which behavioural changes they intended to implement as a result of participating in the programme. Once again, the range was predictably diverse. 35% indicated that they would continue to work on behaviours within the domain of the *I-dimension*. But 39% indicated that they needed to make some changes in their use of the *You-dimension*, and another 35% said that for them they needed to work on effective use of the *We-dimension*. (Some respondents wished to work on more than one dimension, so the total adds up to more than 100%.)

We find this noteworthy, because it is very rare indeed that we have a participant who is able to say at the beginning of a programme that he or she needs to work on sharing feelings, disclosing needs, or acknowledging others. But all the comments cited above seem to reflect, in one way or another, insights related to connecting with others, which is what the *You-dimension* and *We-dimension* are all about. This confirms our deep-seated belief in the importance of trust and the creation of strong relationships in organisations.

Non-Western Experiences

The traditions on which our work is built are very western, mainly American and northern European. Most of the participants we have had the privilege of working with were

Western European, and most Asians we met were, by and large, very westernised through university education and work experience. But we have also been fortunate enough to be able to work with twelve groups in Bangalore as well as with groups in Shanghai, Hong Kong and Singapore. Though the client organisation was Western, we were very unsure how transposable our programme was to different cultures. To our delight it was extremely well received. At the close of a programme in Hong Kong one participant even said:

"The person who designed this programme must have been a genius."

Even allowing for some exaggeration we were very happy that the programme and the concepts worked so well.

Frank Garten, a colleague who specialises in the complexities of working across cultures, regularly uses our behavioural model when facilitating difficult communication processes and negotiations. Concerning his experience, he wrote:

The model works well regardless of which culture it is applied in, if sufficient time (which is dependent on the culture) is provided to build a trusting climate. Cultural factors determine how emotions are experienced and whether or not it is socially acceptable to show certain emotions. There are differences in the way in which certain aspects of the model are experienced. But the three dimensions are always of importance for successful communication and cooperation.[53]

---

[53]From an email exchange with the authors. See also Frank Garten: *Werken met andere culturen*, 2011.

Building an open and supportive learning climate requires extra time in the Far East. Asking people to provide feedback is more problematical in a culture in which loss of face must be avoided at all costs. It takes time for strangers to be admitted to the circle of intimates. But once the barriers have broken down – as always happens – the participants embrace the content and the exercises with enthusiasm. Working with the influence model successfully requires some adjustments, but it is recognisable to and useful for everyone.

We learned that individuals in India are extremely hard working (ten-to twelve-hour days are a norm), very ambitious and very task-focused. They frequently carry responsibility for an extended family, and therefore have very little time for themselves. It was striking how frequently the opportunity to take time for themselves and reflect was highlighted on evaluation forms.

We also experienced that a higher percentage of participants than in Europe made use of the opportunity to have a one-on-one consultation with a facilitator, and the issues raised by them were often of a very personal nature, not directly related to programme issues. They relished the opportunity to talk about themselves, about their lives and the challenges they faced. What they often missed in their lives was real connection with others – outside the extended family of course.

In Shanghai, Hong Kong and Singapore, as well as in the United States, we unfortunately had to make an exception to our practice of conducting the programme on a residential basis. At the end of a day the participants rushed home to their families, which are so important in their culture. We also found Asian participants to be solution-oriented: they wanted to know what to do in specific situations from day one. But once they started to understand what type of learning environment they were in, so different from anything they had experienced before, they took to it with great enthusiasm. They opened up to each other, became less teacher-dependent, gave and received excellent feedback and challenged each other to experiment with new behaviours. They sometimes described it all as a magical experience.

We end this final chapter with a detailed account of one participant's "magic moment".

Suddenly he could hardly hold back his tears any longer. Embarrassed by this, he excused himself and left the room. Nobody followed – something for which he was very grateful. He left the hotel and headed off blindly into the busy streets of the town. He walked without seeing where he went, trying to avoid the possible stares of passers-by.

He asked himself why he was feeling so emotional, and found himself in a black hole of disempowerment, of inability. Back in the hotel, in a small room with a number of other participants, he had discovered that he couldn't do what for some others appeared to be the simplest things: saying what he wanted, giving direct and confronting feedback, standing up for himself. He couldn't understand why this was so impossible for him. What's more, if he couldn't manage these things for himself, how could he ever help others to empower themselves? How could he ever help others to learn if he couldn't learn himself? He felt himself to be small and weak.

Walking further, the emotions subsided and a certain hesitant calm returned. He started to recognise that this inability, this feeling of powerlessness, was probably something which afflicted others as well, maybe even all others, though in different ways. If only he could accept himself, then he would be so much better able to accept others, and maybe that was what he needed to do above all. Didn't everyone come here to wrestle with him – or herself? If not that, why would they be here in the first place? Learning is not always fun, it sometimes means enduring pain, occasionally of a very intense sort.

After about two hours of wandering he found his way back to the hotel and, a little sheepishly, re-entered the room. People looked up and one or two asked if he was okay. Still a little embarrassed he said he was, thank you – and indeed he was. Much better.

The year in which this took place was 1977. The participant was one of the authors of this book. The trainers were Roger Harrison and David Berlew.

BEHAVIOUR

QUESTIONNAIRE

Please read the introduction on page 73, Chapter 2 before proceeding. You may photocopy these pages for your own use.

Completed by: About:

Below you will find a number of statements organised into three groups. Score the statements between 1 (low) and 5 (high):

- Score with a 4 or 5 if the person does this frequently and well.
- Score with a 1 or 2 if the person does this not at all or little, or ineffectively.

BEHAVIOUR QUESTIONNAIRE

Group 1

☐ Indicates clearly whether he/she agrees with something or not.

☐ Tries to convince others with energy and conviction.

☐ Expresses his/her expectations clearly when requesting something.

☐ Expresses his/her views and opinions clearly.

☐ States clearly what he/she will do or not do.

☐ Gives clear reasons for supporting or rejecting an idea or proposal.

☐ States clearly what is at stake or important.

☐ Takes strong initiatives in a discussion.

Group 2

☐ Invites others to express their views, opinions or feelings.

☐ Permits silence, giving others time to think.

☐ Asks follow-up questions in an interested and inviting manner.

☐ Remains calm and patient when others are speaking.

☐ Is attentive to the wishes and expectations of others.

☐ Responds to what others say.

☐ Conveys sincere interest in others' views.

☐ Actively checks whether he/she has understood others properly.

Group 3

☐ Is open about own needs and feelings.

☐ Is open about own doubts and uncertainties.

☐ Demonstrates respect for and acceptance of others" views, even in the face of strong differences.

☐ Is able to put self in someone else's position, to
empathise.

☐ Is open to discussing the way in he/she and others work
together.

☐ Takes others' opinions and feelings seriously.

☐ Gives others his/her full attention.

☐ Shows it clearly when in need of support or help.

Comments (optional):

_____

Copy the scores you received from yourself and others into the
tables below, and add the totals. Analyse the results using the
suggestions on page 73, Chapter 2. Make notes on the
following page.

Group 1: *I-dimension*
Self

☐ ☐ ☐ ☐ ☐ Indicates clearly whether he/she agrees
with something or not.

☐ ☐ ☐ ☐ ☐ Tries to convince others with energy and
conviction.

☐ ☐ ☐ ☐ ☐ Expresses his/her expectations clearly
when requesting something.

☐ ☐ ☐ ☐ ☐ Expresses his/her views and opinions
clearly.

☐ ☐ ☐ ☐ ☐ States clearly what he/she will do or not
do.

☐ ☐ ☐ ☐ ☐ Gives clear reasons for supporting or rejecting an idea or proposal.

☐ ☐ ☐ ☐ ☐ States clearly what is at stake or important.

☐ ☐ ☐ ☐ ☐ Takes strong initiatives in a discussion.

☐ ☐ ☐ ☐ ☐ TOTALS

Group 2: *You-dimension*
Self

☐ ☐ ☐ ☐ ☐ Invites others to express their views, opinions or feelings.

☐ ☐ ☐ ☐ ☐ Permits silence, giving others time to think.

☐ ☐ ☐ ☐ ☐ Asks follow-up questions in an interested and inviting manner.

☐ ☐ ☐ ☐ ☐ Remains calm and patient when others are speaking.

☐ ☐ ☐ ☐ ☐ Is attentive to the wishes and expectations of others.

☐ ☐ ☐ ☐ ☐ Responds to what others say.

Conveys sincere interest in others' views.

☐ ☐ ☐ ☐ ☐ Actively checks whether he/she has understood others properly.

☐ ☐ ☐ ☐ ☐ TOTALS

Group 3: *We-dimension*

Self

☐ ☐ ☐ ☐ ☐ Is open about own needs and feelings.

☐ ☐ ☐ ☐ ☐ Is open about own doubts and uncertainties.

☐ ☐ ☐ ☐ ☐ Demonstrates respect for and acceptance of others' views, even in the face of strong differences.

☐ ☐ ☐ ☐ ☐ Is able to put self in someone else's position, to empathise.

☐ ☐ ☐ ☐ ☐ Is open to discussing the way in he/she and others work together.

☐ ☐ ☐ ☐ ☐ Takes others' opinions and feelings seriously.

☐ ☐ ☐ ☐ ☐ Gives others his/her full attention.

☐ ☐ ☐ ☐ ☐ Shows it clearly when in need of support or help.

☐ ☐ ☐ ☐ ☐ TOTALS

NOTES: (Messages, insights, points deserving particular attention, questions which need answering)

Appendix 2

Words for feelings

There are very many words which can be used to express feelings; there are also many ways to categorise them. For example, all feelings can be considered to be variations or shades of four basic feeling "colours": **happy, sad, angry** and **afraid**. A small number of these shades are listed in no particular order in the table below. Bear in mind that everyone at some point experiences mixed feelings: feelings from different columns can be experienced simultaneously.

Happy	**Sad**	**Angry**	**Afraid**
Cheerful	Ashamed	Annoyed	Anxious
Comfortable	Disappointed	Bitter	Apprehensive
Affectionate	Discouraged	Irritated	Fearful
Curious	Downcast	Irate	Frightened
Delighted	Frustrated	Mad	Suspicious
Energised	Lethargic	Upset	Terrified
Grateful	Lonely	Disgusted	Worried
Interested	Miserable	Furious	Bewildered
Involved	Sorrowful	Shocked	Disturbed

Loving	Pessimistic	Agitated	Scared
Optimistic	Unhappy	Impatient	Troubled
Satisfied	Mournful	Jealous	Uncomfortable
Pleased	Dejected	Resentful	Sceptical
Relaxed	Depressed	Dismayed	Uneasy

Words for Needs

Positive feelings reflect the fact that our needs are being met; negative feelings reflect the fact that our needs are not being met. In the workplace and in general social settings some of the most important operative human needs are:

acceptance	honesty
autonomy	inspiration
appreciation	meaning
authenticity	reassurance
closeness	respect
community	safety
consideration	support
ability to contribute	trust
emotional security	understanding
empathy	warmth

PREPARING FOR A DIFFICULT DISCUSSION

It is useful to prepare thoroughly for what might be a difficult discussion or meeting. The following points for consideration can help in this process. Respond to each question briefly, avoiding organisational or technical details. Focus on what matters in terms of influence behaviour and tactics. If possible, check your analysis with a trusted colleague; this person can help to make your approach even more realistic.

1. Who is the other person who is involved? What is your organisational relationship with him or her?
2. What kind of behaviour have you used in the past with this person or this type of person?
3. Which behaviours were effective? Ineffective?
4. Which environmental factors (organisational pressures, conflicts of interest etc.) play a significant role in the situation?

5. What do you wish to achieve in this discussion? Be specific and concrete: you must formulate your objective in such a way that you can know immediately after the meeting whether you have achieved it or not. Select one main objective, because if you seek to achieve too many things at once the risk is great that you will not achieve any.

6. What assumptions are you making about the situation, about the other person or about yourself? Are these assumptions justified? Can you set aside any dubious assumptions? Would a different mind-set help you to be more effective?

7. Can you call to mind a role-model, someone who is really good at dealing with this sort of situation? How does he/she do it, verbally and non-verbally?

8. A meeting usually consist of a number of stages or phases:
   - Introduction: create trust, putting both parties at ease
   - Opening: deciding/agreeing on the meeting's objective
   - Exploration: getting facts on the table, discovering what both party's perceptions of the issue are, determining underlying needs
   - Resolution: formulating proposals, comparing them, selecting one
   - Next steps: planning and agreeing
   - Closing: brief review of meeting, saying goodbye

   On which phase of the meeting do you need to focus during this preparation? Zoom in on this phase through the following questions.

9. If you think of the four levels of communication, which level(s) will you need to be prepared to shift to?

10. Which dimensions will be most important in order to lead a successful discussion? Which behaviours? (Refer to pages 60 to 62.) What non-verbal behaviours will you need to think about?
11. How do you expect the other person to respond (in behavioural terms)? What will you find difficult to deal with? What will you do to deal with the other person's reactions?
12. How will you begin whichever phase of the discussion you have focused on?

BIBLIOGRAPHY

Blake, Robert and Mouton, Jane. 1964. *The Managerial Grid*. Gulf Publishing

Brooks, David. 2011. *The Social Animal: The Hidden Sources of Love, Character, and Achievement*. New York: Random House

Chief Luther Standing Bear. 1991. In *Native American Wisdom* complied by Kent Nerburn and Louise Mengelkoch. Novato, CA: New World Library

Covey, Stephen R. 1990. *The 7 Habits of Highly Effective People*. New York: Simon & Schuster

Epictetus (55 – 135 AD), as cited by Lebell, Sharon. 1994. *Manual for Living*. San Francisco: HarperCollins

Flores, Carlo Fernando. 1982. *Management and Communication in the Office of the Future*. (Unpublished manuscript).

Ford, Debbie. 2001. *The Dark Side of the Light Chasers*. London: Hodder and Stoughton.

Fukayama, Francis. 1995. *Trust: The Social Virtues and the Creation of Prosperity*. New York: Simon & Schuster.

Garten, Frank. 2001. *Werken met Andere Culturen*. Culemborg (The Netherlands): van Duuren Management

Gladwell, Malcolm. 2005. *Blink: The Power of Thinking Without Thinking*. London: Penguin Books.

Glaser, Judith E. 2005. *Creating WE*. Avon, MA: Platinum Press (Adams Media)

Goleman, Daniel. 1995. *Emotional Intelligence*. New York: Bantam Books

Harrison, Roger. 1985. *Consultants' Journey*. London & New York: McGraw-Hill

Harrison, Roger. 1985. Empowerment in Organizations in *Collected Papers*, 1995. London & New York: McGraw-Hill

Hersey, Paul and Blanchard, Robert. 1969. *Management of Organizational Behaviour*. Prentice Hall

Kay, Roselyn. 2010. Trust as a Verb in *Innovation Partners International Newsletter*.

Lencioni, Patrick. 2002. *The Five Dysfunctions of a Team*. San Francisco: Jossey-Bass.

McGregor, Douglas. 1960. *The Human Side of Enterprise*. McGraw-Hill

Mehrabian, Albert. 1972. *Silent Messages*. Wadsworth Publishing Company

Mercier, Pascal. 2008. *Night Train to Lisbon*. London: Atlantic Books.

Miller, Stephen. 2006. *Conversation: A History of a Declining Art*. New Haven and London: Yale University Press.

Putnam, Robert D. 2000. *Bowling Alone: The Collapse and Revival of American Community*. New York; Simon & Schuster.

Rosenberg, Marshall B. 2000. *Nonviolent Communication: A Language of Compassion*. Encinitas, CA: PuddleDancer Press

Ross, Rick. Moments of Awareness. 1994. In *The Fifth Discipline Fieldbook*, ed. by Peter M. Senge *et.al*. London: Nicholas Brealey Publishing

Schulz von Thun, Friedemann. 1994. *Kommunicieren lernen (und umlernen)*. Hahner Verlaggesellschaft.

Searle, John. 1969. *Speech Acts*. Cambridge University Press.

Simons, George. 1989. *Working Together – How to Become more Effective in a Multicultural Organization*. Los Altos, CA: Crisp Publications, Inc.

Solomon, Robert C. & Flores, Fernando. 2001. *Building Trust in Business, Politics, Relationships and Life*. Oxford University Press.

Spence, Jonathan D. 1991. *The Search for Modern China*. W.W. Norton & Co.

Tolle, Eckhart. 2005. *A New Earth*. London: Penguin Books.

Watzlawick, Paul. 1974. *Pragmatics of Human Communication*. New York: W.W. Norton & Company.

Weick, Karl E. 1995. *Sensemaking in Organizations*. London: Sage Publications

Wilson, Timothy D. 2002. *Strangers to Ourselves: Discovering the Adaptive Unconscious*. Cambridge, MA and London: Harvard University Press.

About the Authors

Nico Swaan (1940) studied engineering physics and subsequently philosophy at the University of Toronto. He started his career in the Management Training and Development department at Ontario Hydro, also in Toronto. Nico spent five years with Bureau Zuidema in The Netherlands where he became acquainted with the work of Roger Harrison. For many years he delivered *The Positive Power and Influence Programme* in both Dutch and English. After a brief interval with an English training and consulting group Nico established himself independently in 1981, working first out of England and later out of The Netherlands. He gained extensive experience in Africa and Asia as well as in Europe and North America. Together with Erik Boers he developed the programme *Focus on Influence* and introduced the English-language version to Philips Consumer Electronics and Philips Semiconductors. The success of the programme was a decisive factor in the decision to establish *Learning Consortium*, an international network of trainers and consultants, together with Erik Boers and several other current and past members.

Email: nico@learningconsortium.eu

Erik Boers (1960) studied philosophy and Dutch language and literature at the Free University of Amsterdam. Together with several lecturers he set up a programme on the philosophy of management and organisation, with which he is still associated as guest lecturer. In order to gain practical experience he joined Philips Electronics as a management trainer. He then joined Bureau Zuidema in order to explore the world outside industry. His profession can be summarised as giving shape to interesting discussions which matter, whether these be deep thought experiments or discussions meant to facilitate the achievement of goals together. Erik has worked as independent trainer/consultant since 1997. Together with Jos Kessels he founded *The New Trivium* (*www.hetnieuwetrivium.nl*). Under this flag he facilitates philosophical discourse in organisations. Together with Jos Kessels and Pieter Mostert he published *Free Space: Philosophy in organisations* (2002) and *Free Space: Field Guide to Conversations* (2008). Working with Nico Swaan, former colleague at Bureau Zuidema, he helped to establish *Learning Consortium* and design the successful training programme *Focus on Influence*.

Email: erik@learningconsortium.eu